MERCY COLLEGE

MERCY COLLEGE

Yesterday & Today

ERIC MARTONE & MICHAEL PERROTA

Published by The History Press
Charleston, SC 29403
www.historypress.net

Cover images courtesy of the Mercy College Library Archives.

First published 2013

ISBN 978.1.540232168

Library of Congress CIP data applied for.

Notice: The information in this book is true and complete to the best of our knowledge. It is offered without guarantee on the part of the authors or The History Press. The authors and The History Press disclaim all liability in connection with the use of this book.

Contents

Forewords

Mercy College is one of the most important and successful independent colleges in New York State. The College's history is useful to all persons interested in higher education and its relevance to intellectual achievement and to meeting the needs of society for talented citizens who can succeed in both life and work. During my presidency of Mercy College, Sister Mary Agnes Parrell, RSM, a professor of history, wrote the College's history with my encouragement. I am delighted with this new book about Mercy College, written by Dr. Eric Martone, assistant professor of social studies education, and Professor Michael Perrota, assistant professor of media studies. I believe it is in the same spirit as Sister Mary Agnes's work and will be useful to anyone interested in Mercy College and its long tradition of success for its students and alumni.

I have met with all the presidents of Mercy College since it became a four-year academic institution in 1961, except for Sister Mary Gratia Maher, RSM, who was president when it achieved the right to give bachelor's degrees. Sister Mary Gratia passed away before I came to the College, but I helped perpetuate her memory by having her portrait painted for the College and by recommending that one of the buildings I acquired for the main campus be named for her. I believe that the leadership of Sister Mary Etheldreda Christie, RSM—dean of the College under Sister Mary Gratia and Mercy College's second president—was a major factor in the institution's long-term success. Under Sister Mary Etheldreda's wise stewardship, the College was able to gain regional accreditation from the Middle States Association for the first time and began to grow in size and quality at its new Dobbs Ferry Campus. Her gentle kindness and sense of humor were inspirations to all who knew her.

The Sisters of Mercy gave much to the College and were always very kind to me. I am grateful for all that they did to start Mercy College. They have contributed so much to its success. When Sister Mary Etheldreda left Mercy College to become an official of the Human Rights Commission in New York City, Dr. Helen "Pat" Coogan, who had served as chair of the speech department, became acting president for two years.

The board of trustees subsequently asked me to become the fourth president in 1972 after a national search because of my prior experience in adding new academic programs that were financially viable. I was happy to accept the job as I admired the College's mission. I was the first person in my family to attend college, and I always have appreciated the importance of a good college education for working-class families. Mercy College has always had lower tuition than other independent liberal arts colleges. This tuition policy enables the institution to be one of the best educational bargains in higher education today.

During my time as president, Mercy College made huge enrollment gains (from 1,700 students in 1972 to more than 9,000 undergraduates, plus many graduate students from LIU and Mercy, in 1984), improved academic quality, gained reaccreditation, developed new facilities and started five branch campuses, as well as built financial surpluses and endowment. Our growth in academic quality and service to our students was recognized by former president Gerald R. Ford and the Academy for Educational Development, which cited Mercy College as being one of the most innovative academic institutions in the United States. When I left the presidency of the College in 1984, most of my goals for the institution had been successfully completed.

I believe that each of the presidents of Mercy College who has succeeded me has brought new ideas to the institution, as have the faculty, staff, alumni, board of trustees and students. I am especially impressed with the success of the current president, Dr. Kimberly Cline, who has done much to increase Mercy College's academic reputation for quality. In addition to the institution's many academic accomplishments under her leadership, she has brought financial success, as evidenced by the College's achievement of the coveted "A" rating from Standard & Poor's. I also believe that each of my successors has succeeded in building on the institution's singular mission to serve persons who often are the first generation in college to achieve academic and professional success. I am confident that when Mercy

College's history is written again, perhaps thirty years from now, the College will have continued to stay true to its reputation of helping many people achieve their potential and succeed in life, in work and as citizens.

I am very happy to have had the opportunity to serve the longest term yet of anyone as president of Mercy College during my twelve years in office. I have many happy memories of the College, including my good luck in meeting my wife, Barbara S. Frees, in the cafeteria when she was a new adjunct professor. We had thirty-one years of happiness after our marriage together before her death from cancer in April 2012. My son, Donald, was baptized in the Mercy College Chapel and played in and around many of the College buildings during the last years of my presidency. My daughter, Susan, came later, but she enjoys the many stories I tell of Mercy College. I met many wonderful people who made the institution successful during my years there. Since then, I continue to hear regularly from people with some connection to the College, including some of my former students from my service as a professor. I am grateful for having the opportunity to have worked at Mercy College. I had so much fun, and I was able to meet and work with so many extraordinary people. As we used to say in an old Mercy College advertisement, "Mercy College Is the Place to Be."

I hope that Mercy College and all connected with it will enjoy success in the future for many years.

Dr. Donald Grunewald
President of Mercy College (1972–84), Distinguished Professor (1984–86)
Professor of Strategic Management, Iona College (1986–present)

It is a pleasure to respond to the request from my colleagues Michael Perrota and Eric Martone for a few words of introduction to their book on the history of Mercy College. Similar to Dr. Grunewald, I have met all the presidents of the College over these sixty-plus years. However, I have also worked for every one of them in some capacity, from secretary to faculty to administrator. Each of these leaders, from the Sisters of Mercy in the early years to the men and women since, has brought a unique perspective and made a significant contribution to what Mercy is today.

However, I want to focus on the real story of Mercy College, namely its faculty. Without doubt, Mercy would not have survived without the enthusiasm and commitment to the College's mission demonstrated by these men and women. They have remained strong during hard times—and there were many—and during good times, such as now. They have responded generously and creatively to the challenges presented by the respective presidents. Consider that at different times, these faculty members have dealt with severe budget crunches and the many accompanying sacrifices. As the College expanded, they agreed to travel far and wide to teach at the extension sites/campuses from Yorktown to Brooklyn or in the prisons throughout the southern tier. They have developed new courses and programs appropriate to the ever-diverse Mercy student body, from scholarship recipients to disadvantaged young minorities and from Cuban refugees to immigrants from Latin America, nurses, Vietnam veterans and other adults of all ages. This is the faculty that welcomed the Long Island University Graduate Center to campus and then went on to develop and staff Mercy's own highly competitive graduate programs. This is a faculty that initiated online learning as a major option for students across the curriculum and has seen enrollment grow once again. For these and many other reasons, the Mercy College faculty can be proud of its efforts to meet today's challenges in higher education.

However, I think that this same faculty would also cite the students in accounting for their joy of teaching in classrooms of such diversity. Whether day, night or weekend, the students of Mercy represent a wonderful kaleidoscope of ages, races, ethnicities, languages and religions. They have many needs, and they have many contributions to make to the learning environment. Because of this, Mercy is a wonderful experience for them as well. I think that the best image of the story and success of Mercy College is the variegated parade of students that walks across the stage at commencement each year, as well as the enthusiasm and gratitude of their families.

I hope that all who read this book by Michael Perrota and Eric Martone will come to have a new appreciation for Mercy College and its accomplishments.

Dr. Ann E. Grow
Professor, Mercy College

Preface

The heritage of the past is the seed from which shall come the harvest of the future.
–National Archives Building, Washington, D.C.

From the moment we embarked on this project, we sought to answer one simple question: "How did Mercy College come into existence and evolve into the complex institution that it is today?" Although Mercy's history is a short one as measured against those institutions dating to colonial America or the great universities of Europe, it is a surprisingly rich one. The College launched recent initiatives to safeguard and promote its heritage, especially during its fiftieth- and sixtieth-anniversary celebrations, and the College's library system has taken on the task of cataloguing and organizing our archive.

Building on this growing interest in Mercy's past, we have sought to create a volume for the present and future generations of the Mercy College community. By the time this book comes into print, Mercy will have produced tens of thousands of distinguished alumni and been the home of thousands of current or former employees, as well as have about ten thousand current students. This book is for those members of the faculty, staff, alumni and student body who might occasionally wonder how and why their College has come to be the one that they know and (presumably) love. Everyone in this vast audience, past or present, has been or still is part of an ongoing story; Mercy is still thriving in the twenty-first century. Consequently, the story of Mercy College is a story about people, for the College has thrived due to the devotion of countless students, faculty, staff, alumni, administrators and trustees.

In constructing this account of the history of Mercy College, we have used local newspapers, antique postcards, university catalogues, official publications and press releases, annual reports, yearbooks, departmental brochures, student publications, memos, interviews, ephemera and materials in the Rockefeller Archive Center. We have also been fortunate to be able to make use of Sister Mary Agnes Parrell's early history of Mercy College, which was printed in 1985. Limited to only a few spiral-bound copies, her work served as the foundation for the present volume. Our efforts to impose an artificial sense of order and meaning on hundreds of semesters of events and personalities have been selective, focusing on the people, organizations and events that, in our judgment, are most responsible for, or best illustrate, the transformation of the total institution. As a result, this volume represents our interpretation of the formation and evolution of Mercy College.

Mercy's presidents have been among the most visible individuals involved in shaping the institution that has strived to retain the integrity of its motto, *Inserviendo consumer* ("To be consumed in service"). Consequently, our chapters use their administrations as a means of dividing the chronology of our story of Mercy. The relationship between the College and the community is also an essential element in the history of the College and receives prominent attention.

A review of any of the chapters in this volume will reveal omissions. One volume can hardly do justice to everyone (or everything). To acknowledge everyone who has contributed to the building of Mercy College and to our perception of that task is an impossible endeavor. Furthermore, we cannot provide encyclopedic coverage of all the activities of each department, school (or division), office, club and team that has contributed to the College over its more than sixty years of existence. We hope that our synthesis, far from being the last word, provides a helpful context for those entering the College during the decades to come.

While this history of Mercy is not an official one, since it has not been commissioned by the College, it could not have been completed without the benefaction and cooperation of various members of the College community. We would like to thank Dr. Kimberly Cline, president of Mercy College, for her support and for graciously contributing the afterword to this book. Dr. Alfred Posamentier, dean of the School of Education, was among this project's most ardent supporters during the course of its development. We would like to extend our gratitude to him for helping to make this book a reality.

We would also like to specifically acknowledge and thank the following individuals who provided research assistance and/or offered insightful comments for improvement on the manuscript: Irene Buckley, chief of staff; Bernadette Wade, chief public relations officer; Jessica Baily, associate director, public relations; Virna Wong; Danielle Mastromarino; Mustafa Sakarya, acting director of the Mercy College Library System; Alex Mouyios; Tesse Santoro, head librarian at the Library Learning Commons; Daniel A. Sabol, reference and instruction librarian; and Robert McKenna. We would also like to thank Dr. Ann Grow for reminiscing about Mercy's history with us and contributing a foreword, Doug Otis and everyone who gave time for interviews, former athletic director Neil Judge and Mercy Athletics for its assistance. We would also like to extend our gratitude to the staff and faculty members of the Schools of Education and Liberal Arts, who provided us with encouragement during the writing of this book.

Outside of Mercy College, we would like to thank Whitney Landis, our commissioning editor at The History Press, for her encouragement and patience, as well as our project editor, Ryan Finn; the Sisters of Mercy; Margaret Hogan and Beth Jaffe-Davis, archivists at the Rockefeller Archive Center in Sleepy Hollow, New York, for their research assistance and coordinating permission to publish material from the archive; and Dr. Donald Grunewald of Iona College for sharing his thoughts and memories about his tenure as president of Mercy College and for writing a foreword for this book.

Finally, we would like to thank the administrators, faculty, staff, students and alumni (past and present) who made Mercy a place worth writing about.

Acknowledgements

Rarely does a student realize that when he or she enrolls in a college-level course, it is his or her job to not only learn but to teach as well. I, for one, underestimated the role of reciprocal teaching in 2004 when I walked onto one of the most beautiful college campuses I had ever seen. I was hired to facilitate knowledge, not acquire it. But learn I did, and I discovered that in the classroom, we all grow together.

This is why I dedicate this book to the hundreds of students I have had the pleasure of teaching over the past decade. I have learned so much from all of you. I value every handshake, every message about how your career is progressing and every joke that we have shared. Thank you for keeping me young and inspired.

I also dedicate this book to those who toiled taking pictures and writing the yearbook, newsletters and college newspaper. Your countless hours locked away on a computer, at a typewriter or even with a simple pen and notepad are the reason why a book like this can be published. From one writer to the next, my sincerest thanks in creating a written record of our history.

Lastly, I dedicate this book to those who took the time to speak with reporters and share their stories and those who posed for the pictures and inspired the funny captions. While you didn't think it mattered at the time, current and future students can now glimpse backward and see what once was.

Thank you for your hairstyles and your fashion sense. Your sweaters, your cat-eye glasses and your large boomboxes. Thank you for the crazy clubs you formed and the parties you held. You were truly a staple of your time, and by your participation, you have allowed all generations of Mercy College students to understand that life existed on this campus in your era, that life exists in his or her current era and that life will exist in future eras. You were all very different, and yet you were all very much the same—college students who hopefully understood that in the quest for knowledge and a career, you took an expedition to discover yourself and your inner passions as well.

To Mercy College students, I say laugh hard and study harder. And on some days, you just have to swap it. May the future generations of Mercy College students continue to be inspired by pioneers of the past.

–Michael Perrota

Part of my job at Mercy College is to educate future teachers. During a course I teach on a semiregular basis, I assign my students the task of writing thank-you notes to teachers who made a profound impact on them. Students frequently take their teachers for granted, and teaching may not bear fruit until years later. I benefitted from having excellent teachers throughout my childhood and adolescent years, and my teachers meant a lot to me. At the time, however, I took them for granted, too. I therefore dedicate this book to my teachers, some of whom were Sisters of Mercy, to say a long-overdue "thank you." I hope you are proud.

–Eric Martone

Chapter 1

A Mission of Mercy, 1950–1972

When first we saw the sunlight glimmer
On thy fields and Hudson waters,
We then were kindled by that spirit—
Hearts inflamed as sons and daughters.
Now our voices loud we're raising
Singing out for thee who taught us.

Hail to Mercy-on-the-Hudson
Now we pledge our voices true,
To thyself and to each other,
Loyal to our white and blue.
Ever onward, ever upward,
Alma Mater in thy name,
From Mount Mercy we go forward,
Hearts inspired by thy flame…
–from "Alma Mater" (1962)[1]

The closing of an academic year is usually a time of celebration, a time to reflect and take pride in the achievements of faculty, staff and students. But a hint of sadness marked the end of the spring 1970 semester, as the upcoming commencement exercises at the Dobbs Ferry Campus were going to accompany the departure of retiring faculty member Sister Mary Gratia Maher. Sister Mary Agnes Parrell, a member of the College's founding faculty, often praised her colleague as "the moving spirit," the one who made the dream of Mercy a reality and the sole reason the College ever existed.[2]

Initially established in 1950 in Tarrytown for members-in-training of the Sisters of Mercy, a Roman Catholic religious community, "Mercy Junior College" had already evolved into a growing four-year coeducational institution of higher education. But every great institution begins as a dream. It was Sister Gratia who helped set the sturdy foundation on which the College developed, serving as first dean and president.

Sister Gratia, born Edith Maher in New York City, became a Sister in 1921 at the age of twenty-five. She held degrees from Fordham and the Catholic University of America and had begun her education career as a schoolteacher and administrator. Sister Gratia's photographs and portraits depict a stern, formal individual. Dr. Ann Grow, former Sister and longtime College faculty member and administrator, recalled in an interview that Sister Gratia always "knew what she wanted" and "wanted things to look the right way." But underneath Sister Gratia's stern façade was a caring and selfless woman who sacrificed much to build Mercy College. As Grow recalled, "I believe she came from a comfortable family and loved nice things, which you didn't always have in the convent…It was fun to see how much she enjoyed choosing beautiful china to use for special guests."[3] Years later, Shakespearean scholar and founding faculty member Sister Mary Joannes Christie gave a moving tribute to her former colleague:

> *The dream took form…but took its toll, too. So did her work long into the dark hours, her solitary light brightening the gloom as she plied her work. Patiently, painstakingly (she had infinite patience) she etched and sketched… This woman of ideas and ideals for her sister-students—for Mercy had people of religion in mind as well as the "young ladies" to whom the College opened in 1961—worked to perfect her plan…From its beginning, Mercy set in motion the machinery to fashion scholars, remembering Aristotle, Aquinas and John Henry Newman. Sister Mary Gratia would have her students appreciate the True, the Good, the Beautiful and, to this end, she provided opportunities for enlarging the capacity to recognize and love the genuine, the cultivated, the beautiful in herself and in those she guided…being herself the examples of what she taught. As an administrator, she shone as one who led—but gently—not as a pillar of power but as a leader who brought others to the limelight, content to develop the gifts in those about her. She lavished praise where it was deserved, saw talents and excellence in unsuspected places and encouraged growth in degrees and experiences.*[4]

At the March 13, 1970 board meeting, it was suggested that the College honor Sister Gratia in some way. During the May 26 commencement proceedings, the board's decision was read publicly in the Mount Mercy Chapel:

> *Sister Mary Gratia Maher...has served Mercy College with distinction and zeal since 1950 as faculty member, Chairman of the Department of Religious Studies, as Dean and President of the College...*[I]*n her years at Mercy...*[she] *has displayed the ideals of the College in her own life and work...*[T]*herefore...it* [is] *resolved that as an expression of gratitude for her contribution to higher education and for her capable leadership in the early years of the College, Sister Mary Gratia Maher be declared President Emerita.*[5]

The honor sought to symbolically mark the end of the first chapter of Mercy's history. But this symbolic end assumed a sense of tangibility when Sister Gratia died on July 16. Her life had been dedicated to both Mercy College and the Sisters of Mercy. The stories of both the Sisters and the College's beginnings are intertwined and part of a larger global history that begins not in New York, but across the Atlantic in Ireland.

Mercy in America

Since their founding in 1831, the Sisters of Mercy have become intertwined with the history of Catholic education in the Atlantic world—so much so that in 1994, Ireland redesigned its five-pound note to bear an image of Catherine McAuley, their founder, on the front, with a depiction of a Sister at a classroom chalkboard on the reverse. During their early history, the Sisters were composed of brave women who flouted their era's gender conventions, achieving social power in a male-dominated world by separating themselves from society through religious vows. McAuley, however, never intended to start a religious order.

Born in about 1778 in Ireland, her parents died while she was a child, and she subsequently suffered from poverty and an unstable childhood. She later secured a position as a nurse-companion to a wealthy but childless Quaker couple; they later adopted her. Upon their deaths, McAuley inherited their estate and used her new wealth to help people who had been in her position when she was younger. In 1827, McAuley opened a "House of Mercy" in

Dublin staffed with female friends. The house, which sheltered orphans and women, eventually provided training to help women gain employment. These training programs expanded and became more academic. McAuley and her companions also made visits to the sick and poor. Such actions, however, challenged the conventions of her time.

The Church, and much of the (male) public, did not support female initiatives like McAuley's done outside Church structures. Under pressure from local officials, McAuley formed the Sisters of Mercy to secure long-term support for her mission. The formation of a convent transferred McAuley's wealth to the collective entity of the Sisters of Mercy, thereby removing it from standard patriarchal inheritance structures. Further, by agreeing to become "sisters" rather than formal "nuns," they exploited loopholes in sixteenth-century ecclesiastical laws that required nuns to make solemn, lifelong vows and observe papal cloister.[6]

After McAuley's death in 1841, the Sisters expanded to areas within the English-speaking world, establishing schools, orphanages and hospitals. As part of this exodus, in 1843, Sister Mary Frances Xavier Warde led a cohort of Sisters from Ireland to America, ultimately founding the Sisters of Mercy of the Americas.[7] The Sisters, tending to congregate in urban areas, increasingly focused on the need to further education, which they perceived as a way to transform the lives of those trapped in cycles of poverty because of ethnicity and/or class, especially women and immigrants, many of whom were Irish.[8]

Although the Jesuits founded more Catholic colleges and universities in America than the Sisters of Mercy, the Sisters remain the largest female founding force in the entire arena of higher education.[9] The Sisters directed their educational efforts primarily at poor and working-class individuals who came from backgrounds similar to their own, intentionally forming nonelitist colleges and universities that posed a radical foil to the educational institutions in nineteenth- and early twentieth-century America (like Yale and Harvard), which had strong Protestant roots and catered to American elites.[10]

MERCY JUNIOR COLLEGE IN TARRYTOWN (1950–61)

The Sisters began their work in New York City in the mid-1800s with an orphanage. Later, they spread to other locations. In December 1892, the Sisters acquired the roughly thirty-acre Kingsland estate in Tarrytown.

TABLE 1. COLLEGES AND UNIVERSITIES ESTABLISHED IN THE UNITED STATES BY THE SISTERS OF MERCY

Current Name	Current Location	Founding Date	Ending Date (N/A: still operated by the Sisters of Mercy)
St. Xavier University	Chicago, IL	1846 (began as an academy; became a college in 1915)	N/A
Mount Aloysius College	Cresson, PA	1853 (began as an academy; became a college in 1939)	N/A
Mount St. Agnes College	Baltimore, MD	1890s	became part of Loyola University, Maryland, in the 1970s
Sacred Heart College	Belmont, NC	1892 (began as an academy; became a college in 1937)	closed in 1987
Mercy College of Health Sciences	Des Moines, IA	1899 (began as a nursing school; became a consolidated college in 1994)	N/A
Georgian Court University	Lakewood, NJ	1908	N/A
St. Joseph's College of Maine	Standish, ME	1912	N/A
Mercy College of Ohio	Toledo, OH	1918 (began as a nursing school; became a college in 1992)	N/A
College of St. Mary	Omaha, NE	1923	N/A
Misericordia University	Dallas, PA	1924	N/A
Trinity College	Burlington, VT	1925	closed in 2000
Mercyhurst University	Erie, PA	1926	N/A
Mount Mercy University	Cedar Rapids, IA	1928	N/A
Carlow University	Pittsburgh, PA	1929	N/A
St. Joseph College	West Hartford, CT	1932	N/A
Mount St. Mary College	Hooksett, NH	1934	closed in 1978
Salve Regina University	Newport, RI	1934 (date of charter; opened in 1947)	N/A
Edgecliff College	Cincinnati, OH	1935	became part of Xavier University in 1980
Mercy College of Detroit	Detroit, MI	1941	consolidated with Detroit University in 1990 to form the University of Detroit Mercy
Gwynedd–Mercy College	Gwynedd Valley, PA	1948	N/A
Mercy College	Dobbs Ferry, NY	1950	became independent and nonsectarian in 1969
Russell College	Burlingame, CA	1950s	now closed
Catherine McAuley Junior College	Rochester, NY	1950s	closed during the 1970s–1980s period
Mercy Junior College	St. Louis, MO	1950s	closed during the 1970s
Our Lady of Mercy College	Auburn, CA	1950s	now closed
Trocaire College	Buffalo, NY	1958	N/A
Maria College	Albany, NY	1958	N/A
Castle College	Windham, NH	1963	closed in 1999
Marian Court College	Swampscott, MA	1964	N/A

In 1850, Ambrose Kingsland, wealthy merchant and former New York City mayor, built a mansion on part of this land, which became known as Wilson Park after nineteenth-century New York City merchant William Wilson built a mansion in the area. Shortly after acquiring the estate, the Sisters discovered remnants of colonial slave quarters on their property's northern end dating from when Tarrytown formed part of the roughly fifty-thousand-acre seventeenth-century Philipsburg Manor, which spanned the Hudson from the Bronx through Westchester County.[11] The property housed an orphanage before transitioning to a school. The Sisters eventually opened Our Lady of Victory Academy (OLVA) there in 1945.

The New York province of the Sisters of Mercy became preoccupied with managing hospitals and schools. However, to be qualified to staff these institutions, the young Sisters needed an education. They often studied for credit granted from neighboring Catholic colleges. A 1938 thank-you letter from Sister Mary Gertrude, supervisor of schools, to their neighbor, John D. Rockefeller Jr., for a library donation detailed this arrangement. After explaining that the new books would aid Sisters in training, she informed Rockefeller:

> *It may interest you to know that our future teachers spend at least two and one-half years at Tarrytown. During that time, in addition to their religious training, the potential teachers receive training in secular subjects. Each Sister destined for the schools completes two years of college work. This...includes courses that are usually given at Normal Training Schools. However, the work done here is accredited college work. After leaving Tarrytown, the Sister who continues study does so on the third year level at college.*[12]

The cost of supplying external educations to all Sisters proved costly. Consequently, the province's superior charged Sister Gratia with creating a local Mercy institution of higher education to educate their order's younger members. As one Sister who worked with Sister Gratia recalled, "Leaders somehow always rise from out [of] their time. In fact, they stand above time. Such a scholar was Sister Mary Gratia."[13] While finishing her doctoral dissertation examining religious instruction at Catholic colleges for women, she assumed responsibilities for planning the new College's curriculum, its organization and the hiring of its faculty. These efforts paralleled similar expansion developments at other Mercy convents that made educating Sisters a priority before placing them in the field. Consequently, Mercy

This postcard from the Hugh C. Leighton Company, circa 1912, depicts the Tarrytown-on-Hudson home of the Sisters of Mercy. The property was composed primarily of two buildings: the Sisters' convent, housed in the former Kingsland mansion (located to the right), and the school building (located to the left). Mercy College was founded as a junior college on this site in 1950. *Private collection of E. Martone.*

A side view of the former Kingsland mansion on the Sisters' Tarrytown property. It was in the back rooms (located to the right) where the first Mercy classes were held. *Sisters of Mercy Archive/Mercy College Library Archives.*

A close-up of the school building on the Sisters' Tarrytown property. This building served as the original home of Our Lady of Victory Academy, which opened in 1945. *Sisters of Mercy Archive/Mercy College Library Archives.*

Junior College was one of the five "Sister Formation Colleges" that opened during the 1950s.[14]

Mercy Junior College began operations as a non-degree-granting institution offering programs at the junior college level (although an interim credit agreement was negotiated with the Catholic University of America). The College's first classes began on September 18, 1950; this date is recorded as the "Founding Date." The initial faculty included Reverend Anselm Burke, Sister Mary Assumpta Knobbe, Sister Mary Carmela Driscoll, Sister Mary Clara Huertos, Sister Mary Etheldreda Christie, Sister Mary Joannes Christie, Sister Gratia, Sister Mary Hilda Leonard, Sister Mary Hugh Cunningham, Reverend Joseph Killeen, Sister Mercia O'Connell, Sister Mary Rosalia Dordoni, Sister Mary Salome White and Sister Mary Agnes Parrell. Helen Coogan and Reverend Richard Curtin helped with special services and music.[15]

Over the next few years, the College expanded. Some new faculty members came from other Catholic institutions, like Dr. Joseph Sherlock from Fordham, while others came from the clergy. In 1951, Father Daniel

Sister Mary Regina (second from left), Sister Mary Jeanne (third from left) and Sister Mary Gratia Maher (third from right) pose with early Mercy graduates at Tarrytown. *Mercy College Library Archives.*

Peake took over the course on Christian doctrine and became a prominent figure at the College. Dr. William Fordrung, whose niece was a Sister, also became a popular professor of philosophy and supporter of the College. He arranged and financed many field trips and made several donations to the College.[16]

On October 23, 1952, the New York State Board of Regents granted the College a charter authorizing its programs of studies for Mercy community members leading to associate's degrees. Several schools—like Manhattan College, Mount St. Vincent College and St. John's University—offered Mercy's seniors scholarships to continue their studies. Mercy's academic programs continued to evolve. For example, Dr. Roy De Ferrari, secretary general of the Catholic University, helped launch Mercy as a center for teacher training. As a result of the establishment of a speech center at the College in 1959 with the help of the director of the archdiocesan speech clinic, the subject received emphasis in the teacher education program.[17]

During the late 1950s, Sister Gratia continued to work with New York State officials to establish Mercy as a four-year women's college and filed a request to become "Mercy College." During the College's early years, the Rockefellers seem to have been unaware it existed, likely because it served only Sisters. Sometime during the mid-1950s, the Sisters decided to open the College to lay women. In 1956, they unsuccessfully petitioned John D. Rockefeller Jr.'s son, Nelson Rockefeller, who also lived nearby, for financial assistance with their plans to develop a women's college. It seems that the Sisters initially contemplated accepting lay women into their existing junior college to complement OLVA's secondary education programs before deciding to relaunch Mercy as a four-year institution. The New York Board of Regents had approved the proposed College "in principle" and gave the Sisters a "time limit" on the verge of expiration to meet their requirements, one of the most significant of which was an expanded physical facility.[18] When Rockefeller Jr. heard about the plan, he became concerned over his property's privacy and contemplated offering the Sisters more than $1 million to build a college elsewhere.[19] By 1960, the board of regents had approved an amendment to the charter authorizing the requested changes, including the ability to confer bachelor's degrees.

During the 1950s, the Sisters also began to search for a new location to support their expanding educational endeavors. Sister Mary Jeanne Ferrier, provincial of the Mercy community, revealed in a private letter that the Sisters had long realized that their Tarrytown property was inadequate "because of size, character of land and obsolescence of the buildings. The present structures do not lend themselves to either modernizing or expansion of facilities. There is not enough land available near the present site for further expansion and after investigation we have discovered that economically we could not provide for our needs if we remain here."[20] During their quest, the Sisters examined about ten sites. In 1956 and 1957, they came close to acquiring properties in Cortlandt and Scarborough, respectively.[21] News that the Sisters were searching for a new location reached Rockefeller Jr. He expressed interest to his agent in negotiating to buy the Sisters' property if the opportunity presented itself. The Rockefellers had been trying to acquire the property, which was across from Kykuit, the main Rockefeller estate, on and off since 1911. Rockefeller Jr.'s agent advised him to offer a substantial gift to ensure the Sisters' move in addition to the property's "fair market value."[22]

In July 1957, the Sisters successfully bid $350,000 for the eighty-five-acre former Edwin Gould estate in Dobbs Ferry.[23] Now that the Sisters had found a new location, they needed to sell their Tarrytown property. Rockefeller Jr. authorized his representatives to negotiate with the Sisters, capping his price at $1.75 million, an amount based on his estimate to reconstruct the Sisters' facility and the "fair market value" of the property (about $150,000). The Sisters, however, wanted a personal commitment from Rockefeller Jr. before proceeding to purchase the Gould estate.[24] In March 1958, Sister Mary Jeanne wrote him a heartfelt letter:

> *During the years since the Sisters of Mercy have been located on the property at Wilson Park, the organization has grown tremendously. For a long period of time it has been realized that the property is inadequate for our use... Therefore, it is our decision to relocate. We have been searching for a suitable site for over a two-year period, and since the Gould property in Dobbs Ferry appears to meet our requirements, it seems very desirable. In order to pursue this further with a view to negotiating for its purchase, we are appealing to you, our good neighbor of many years, to assist us that we may continue our charitable endeavors for humanity. The expansion program that we are considering will involve a huge expenditure far beyond our normal capacity. The accomplishment of this will not be possible unless we can secure the market sale price for our Tarrytown site and a substantial donation over and above. Aware of your manifold charities and your genuinely sincere interest in education and social welfare agencies, it is with confident hope that I present our needs to you.*[25]

After drafting several versions of a response, in April he finally sent Sister Mary Jeanne the following letter of pledge:

> *I have received your very kind and gracious letter of March 25 relative to the expansion program of the Sisters of Mercy. You say that due to your tremendous growth and the limitations of your present property you have been forced to look elsewhere...and you have found in the Gould property at Dobbs Ferry the suitable site that will answer your requirements. In view of the pleasant and neighborly relations which have existed for so many years between the Sisters and the members of our family, I...am now confirming...*[my representative, Mr. William Yates's] *verbal commitment to you on my behalf—namely, that on your assurance that you have acquired title to the Gould property...and that you will immediately proceed with the erection thereon of buildings required by your institution, I agree to contribute to the Institution of Mercy securities having a market value of $1,600,000 at the time of delivery.*[26]

This early twentieth-century postcard from the Collotype Company depicts the view of the Hudson from the Gould mansion in Dobbs Ferry, in the vicinity of the future site of Mercy Hall. *Private collection of E. Martone.*

The Sisters' plans, however, were almost derailed by a dispute between the Catholic Church and the local board of education over the Sisters' desired property. The board felt that the Gould property was the only adequate land available in Dobbs Ferry for a new school needed to resolve overcrowding issues. It wanted the Sisters to reduce the amount of property they intended to purchase. The Sisters, however, intended to sell part of the estate to the Sacred Heart Catholic Church for a parochial school. Francis Spellman, cardinal and archbishop of New York, opposed the school board in the press, claiming that a parochial school would resolve the overcrowding issue.[27] Several local referendums resulted in decisions favoring the Sisters, and the matter was put to rest.

The agreement of sale between Rockefeller Jr. and the Sisters for their Tarrytown property (about 10 percent of which technically resided in Sleepy Hollow) was signed in May 1958. He paid the Sisters with 32,200 shares of Standard Oil and received the title on August 19.[28] The Sisters also completed their transaction to acquire the Gould property in August.[29] However, Rockefeller Jr. asked the Sisters to keep his $1.6 million gift a secret until later in the year, in part to boost Nelson Rockefeller's underdog campaign for governor with positive press.[30] Consequently, the gift was not announced until October.

The press gave significant coverage to the donation and its intended use for the construction of a new complex, Mount Mercy-on-the-Hudson.[31] The complex cost nearly $7 million. In comparison, the price of an average house was under $20,000. The complex included Mercy College, OLVA, the provincial house, the mother house (with a convent, infirmary, novitiate and juniorate for Sisters of first vows, forming the wings of "a polygonal chapel") and a parish elementary school.[32] The press, however, sometimes incorrectly referred to the College as "Mount Mercy College."[33] That same month, no longer obligated to conceal their abundant gratitude, the Sisters sent a token of their appreciation to their "esteemed benefactor": a framed manuscript stating that "each of the four hundred Sisters of Mercy of the Province of New York, in deep and sincere gratitude, has offered to God one day of Prayer Labor Sacrifice in the spiritual and corporal works of mercy." It concluded with a quote from Ephesians 3:6–19.[34]

Meanwhile, Rockefeller Jr. leased to the Sisters their former Tarrytown property for $1. The two-year lease called for the Sisters to purchase insurance to protect two cottages on the property that he wanted to keep. It also contained a provision allowing for an extension on a month-to-month basis "if, after…due diligence, the tenant is unable to complete the construction of such new buildings."[35] The Sisters continued to seek donations for the Mercy Building Fund and even secured an anonymous $1,000 donation from Nelson Rockefeller.[36]

The Move to Dobbs Ferry (1961–70)

On December 9, 1959, the Sisters signed a contract to begin the complex's construction, which was scheduled to be completed in 550 days. Consequently, Sister Mary Jeanne informed Rockefeller Jr. that the Sisters intended to move by July 1961.[37] The Mount Mercy groundbreaking ceremony on December 12, 1959, coincided with the 114th anniversary of the Sisterhood's founding in Manhattan. Malcolm Wilson, lieutenant governor, gave the principal address. Other attendees included Sister Mary Jeanne, councilor general of the Sisters; Sister Mary Regina Haughney, mother vicar provincial; Monsignor John Voight, secretary of education to Cardinal Spellman; and Reverend John Maguire, auxiliary bishop of New York.[38] Wilson, who eventually became governor in 1973, remained a strong supporter of the College and returned to the campus to give commencement addresses in

1966 and 1982. During his second address, he alluded to his role at the groundbreaking while reflecting on the institution's early history:

> *More than I suspect many of you know, 1827 in Dublin Ireland marked the beginning of the Sisters of Mercy...The New York Province...was established in 1846 and I was present at the 100th Anniversary in 1946 in St. Patrick's Cathedral, New York City. The Mother House of the New York Province stood in Tarrytown diagonally across the road from the Pocantico Hills estate of the Rockefeller family. As a matter of fact, when I first started going up to see the Governor and later* [U.S.] *Vice President* [Nelson Rockefeller], *I entered the grounds by way of what was then known as "the Sister's Gate." In 1950 a college, not for general registration but for members of the order, provided higher education for the Sisters. By the late 1950s it was very evident that they would have to serve a larger constituency. Not only did Mr. Rockefeller, notably John D. Rockefeller, Jr., purchase the house and all the buildings and grounds but also provided a very generous gift that made it possible to move Mercy College to Dobbs.*[39]

As the complex's construction got underway, Sister Mary Jeanne continued to correspond with Rockefeller Jr. During the negotiations to sell the Sisters' Tarrytown property, she made a favorable impression on him—he described her in private as "wise, able and gracious"—and on his associates, one of whom perceived her as "quite a business lady."[40] Consequently, she and Rockefeller Jr. developed a sense of respect for each other. As she confided to him in one letter, "The plans for our new Mount Mercy [complex]...are rapidly approaching completion...Eight buildings present a challenge to one's mental efforts as the endeavor is made to avoid any and all mistakes which might arise from insufficient consideration. This is a tremendous project and we shall always be grateful to you. It embodies our prayers, hopes and dreams for an expansion of our facilities that will enable us to work ever more effectively for...the underprivileged of our country and in particular of our eastern area."[41] In April 1960, shortly before his death, she sent him an Easter card, calling him a "friend and benefactor" and urging his recovery.[42]

The site on which the Sisters' new complex was being developed was one of historical importance. Located within the site was Wickers Creek, a stream that flows into the Hudson. The Wekquaesgeeks, an Amerindian tribe, had maintained a village on the Mount Mercy property around this creek. Consequently, in the 1970s, Mount Mercy's southern boundary was

The New

Mount Mercy on-the-Hudson

Dobbs Ferry, N. Y.

Ceremony of Ground Breaking

- Our Lady of Victory Academy
- Mercy College
- Residence for Student Sisters
- Faculty Residence
- Residence for Senior Sisters
- Provincialate
- Chapel

Saturday, December 12, 1959

Foundation Day of the Sisters of Mercy

The cover of the program for the groundbreaking ceremony of the Mount Mercy-on-the-Hudson complex. *Mercy College Library Archives.*

designated a Westchester Landmark.[43] During the American Revolution, British and American forces likely made camps at different times near Wickers Creek. In 1781, George Washington established his headquarters at Dobbs Ferry. A French army under General Comte de Rochambeau landed in Rhode Island in 1780 and made a valiant trek through Connecticut in 1781 to rendezvous with Washington. The Franco-American force subsequently began its celebrated march from Dobbs Ferry toward Yorktown and victory.[44] The troops gathered near Mount Mercy on what is now Route 9, originally an Amerindian footpath that became known over time as King's Highway, Queen's Highway, Highland Turnpike, Albany Post Road and, finally (after 1850), Broadway.

Edwin Gould eventually established a residence on the property during the early twentieth century. As one historian recounted, Gould built "a forty-room mansion of Spanish architecture with a red tile patio in front of the main house. A bluestone gatehouse stood at the Broadway entrance where the Sacred Heart School [now the Alcott Montessori School] was later erected. There were thirteen smaller buildings besides the main house on the estate," which became known as Agawam.[45] Gould—son of Jay Gould, the "robber baron" who had relocated to Lyndhurst in Tarrytown—earned his father's disfavor when he withdrew from Columbia. However, he redeemed himself after making more than $1 million in six months by speculating in railroads. Edwin Gould's mother-in-law was involved in charity work, especially for orphans. He began to assist her efforts, especially after his twenty-three-year-old son's tragic death.[46] In 1923, he established the Edwin Gould Foundation for Children, which continued after his death in 1933 and gave property and funds to the village in 1924 to create Gould Park.[47] At the time of his death, *Time* wrote of him:

> *His brothers and sisters...all insisted on marrying actresses or noblemen—generally more than once...Not only the publicity of these affairs rose to trouble Edwin Gould but the legal entanglements arising from them...All this was as distressing to Edwin Gould as the unanimity with which historians described his father as the greatest and most wicked pirate of the buccaneering age in U.S. industry. But he modestly went his way, made and gave away his modest millions, died without ostentation, of a sudden heart attack.*[48]

Gould's charity work, care for children and interest in the community made his former estate a suitable site for the Sisters' new complex, which was nearing completion in the fall of 1961. That year, the Sisters moved from Tarrytown to Mount Mercy. Meanwhile, the main buildings on their former Tarrytown property were razed. During the early twenty-first century, construction companies purchased the site of Mercy's original campus and, despite local opposition, built luxury homes on the property near the intersection of Wilson Park Drive and County House Road.[49]

Sister Mary Salome White, whom Sister Mary Agnes Parrell notes in her early history of Mercy College as the last president of the College at its Tarrytown location, during the late 1960s. *Mercy College Library Archives.*

Sister Gratia became the first president and dean of Mercy College during the transition from Tarrytown to Dobbs Ferry (and from junior college to four-year college status). The move, which occurred throughout September and October, was difficult because the construction of the complex's eight brick buildings (of "contemporary architecture" designed by York and Sawyer of New York) was delayed by the Stewart Muller Construction Company, which was based in White Plains. The College building, for example, was incomplete. Sister Mary Daniel Brackett, principal of OLVA, which

Mount Mercy-on-the-Hudson during the 1960s. *Mercy College Library Archives.*

A photograph depicting "move-in day" to the new Mount Mercy complex. As the photograph reveals, the site was not completed on schedule. *Sisters of Mercy Archives/Mercy College Library Archives.*

Our Lady of Victory Academy was a crucial component of the Mount Mercy complex. Mercy College's first classes at Dobbs Ferry were held in this building because of construction delays. After the academy closed in 2011, its building became part of Mercy College's Dobbs Ferry Campus as Victory Hall. *Photograph by E. Martone.*

The Mercy College Building as it originally appeared in the early 1960s. Several additions have been made to this building, now Main Hall, during Mercy's history. The largest addition, an entire right wing, was constructed from 1965 to 1968 and doubled the size of the original facility. *Mercy College Library Archives.*

had been completed, permitted Mercy's freshman class to temporarily use the academy for classes. In December 1961, the first capping ceremony finally occurred in Spellman Auditorium.[50] Sister Gratia had recruited the top female students from regional Catholic parishes and schools for the College's entering class, enticing them with full scholarships and perceiving them as a long-term investment in the College's academic reputation. She realized that when these students graduated in 1965, they would become the College's representatives. What the outside world made of these early alumnae would affect the College's academic reputation and its ability to attract top students.[51]

Mount Mercy's dedication ceremony did not occur until May 20, 1962. Cardinal Spellman presided over the dedication, blessing the complex. Nelson Rockefeller, now governor, participated in the ceremony. As the Rockefellers' representative, he received the Sisters' public expressions of gratitude on behalf of his late father, who had recently died.[52]

After guiding the College through its first year of transition, Sister Gratia, due to impaired health, resigned as president. She decided to remain, however, as a faculty member. Consequently, Sister Mary Etheldreda Christie became College president in 1962. Known for her warmth and charisma, she was well respected by her colleagues, one of whom described her as

There are few photographs documenting the 1962 dedication ceremony of the Mount Mercy complex. In this photograph, prominent Sisters involved in the founding of the College—including Sister Mary Regina Haughney (second from right) and Sister Mary Jeanne Ferrier (far left)—pose with Sister Mary Regina, Mother General (second from left), Sister Mary Eymard (far right) and Francis Spellman, cardinal and archbishop of New York. *Mercy College Library Archives.*

"gifted by nature," a leader who "walked the heights and generously helped others to arrive there." A graduate of Manhattan College and Fordham, she was already a veteran educator and administrator. In her early history of Mercy, Sister Agnes praised Sister Etheldreda, claiming that the steady building of the College during the 1960s "was the result of a single minded,

A group of Sisters exits the College Building (Main Hall) during the 1960s. *Mercy College Library Archives.*

Previous, bottom: This second photograph from the 1962 dedication ceremony of the Mount Mercy complex depicts (from left to right) Cardinal Spellman; Governor Nelson Rockefeller; and Reverend John Maguire, vicar general of the Archdiocese of New York and chancellor of Mercy College. *Mercy College Library Archives.*

Sister Elizabeth Pogue with the College's early international students, a cohort of Sisters from Kerala, India, during the 1960s. *Mercy College Library Archives.*

carefully planned efforts of a very warm-hearted person." Her leadership oversaw enormous institutional transformation and "inspired community spirit and common purpose in her students, faculty, and staff."[53] She was also fortunate to be assisted by the exceptionally talented dean of the College, Sister Frances Mahoney.

While working to improve the College, Sister Etheldreda worked closely with its board, which, during the 1960s, became composed of three laymen and nine Sisters (three from the Provincial Council, three from the College administration and three from the New York province at large). One prominent trustee, Sister Theresa Kane (appointed in 1966), became famous in 1979 when she confronted Pope John Paul II about gender inequality in the Catholic Church during his papal visit to Washington, D.C. Prominent lay board members included Walter Danaher, principal of Dobbs Ferry High School; Eugene Hult, Yonkers resident and deputy superintendent of New York City public schools; William Stoutenburgh, a retired New York investment broker from New Jersey; and Malcolm Wilson. In December 1970, Joan Demarest became the first Mercy alumnus to serve on the board.[54]

During the early 1960s, the number of Mercy students and faculty remained modest. In 1962, for example, Mercy could boast only seventy-nine students. In 1963, the College's faculty activities report listed only twenty-seven faculty members. By the mid-1960s, however, freshman classes regularly numbered over one hundred. To allow for greater enrollment, the auditorium became a cafeteria, and the "tearoom" became a lecture hall. The Admissions Office launched new recruitment efforts to encourage continued growth. An admissions committee held "College Nights" in local schools and open-house events. Potential students were also treated to "Go to College Days." Consequently, enrollment surged to about six hundred full-time students during the 1966–67 academic year. With a growing student body and academic prestige, international specialists came to teach at Mercy. For example, the "scholarly" Sister Mary Madeleine came from England to teach the history of the English language.[55]

Enrollment increases necessitated an expansion of facilities. Therefore, almost as soon as Mercy opened, it launched new construction projects. With Nelson Rockefeller's assistance, the College secured a New York Dormitory Authority loan to build an addition in 1965 to the College

Mercy Hall during the 1960s. Note the church bell above the entrance. *Mercy College Library Archives.*

Christmas Mass at the Mount Mercy Chapel (the Rotunda) during the 1960s. *Mercy College Library Archives.*

Building. In one of her reports to the board, Sister Etheldreda cited the "building expansion" as the issue "looming largest" in the year. She hoped that the construction of the new academic wing and dining facilities would soon commence. The addition, completed in 1968, doubled the original facility's size. Plans were also made in 1966 to enlarge the library, which then included a modest fifty thousand volumes, as the result of the Sisters being willed a sum of $40,000.[56]

Sister Etheldreda's presidency included external recognition of the College's excellence. The New York Board of Regents issued Mercy an absolute charter in 1965. Later, in 1968, the College gained accreditation. Sister Etheldreda welcomed a laudatory letter dated May 6 from Frank Piskor, chair of the Middle States Association, informing her that "the Commission has voted to accredit Mercy College. This is a milestone for you and a proud moment

Above: One of the early graduation ceremonies at the Mount Mercy complex. The first commencement guest speaker at the Dobbs Ferry Campus was Dr. Edward J. Mortola, president of Pace College (now Pace University). Eventually, the College's student body became too large for such an intimate graduation setting, and it had to be held elsewhere. *Mercy College Library Archives.*

Right: Sister Mary Constance Golden replaced Sister Mary Regina Haughney as chair of the College's board of trustees during Mercy's bid for initial accreditation from Middle States. *Mercy College Library Archives.*

for us, and I am personally pleased to have the honor of welcoming you to membership in the Middle States Association."[57]

However, Mercy did not rest on its laurels. During the late 1960s, it launched several new academic initiatives. In 1968, the New York State Education Department approved Mercy's provision for training veterans under the Veterans Readjustment Benefits Act (1966). Further, the College launched a Continuing Education Program for older adults. Mercy initiated a program for foreign students, especially Cubans fleeing Communist Cuba, to receive U.S. certification for professions for which they had been licensed in their native lands. Mercy also forged a role as a "place of intellectual adventure." The College initiated a conference series on contemporary culture. The first, on India and China, occurred in 1963 and included international dignitaries and professors from Columbia and Fordham Universities.[58]

Meanwhile, the first lay students formed a thriving campus life, which included a renowned glee club, exciting theater productions, social clubs, honor societies and an annual beach party. Mercy also had an active anti–Vietnam War unit.[59] In a letter to Sister Agnes, alumna Patricia Williams Fitzgerald painted a vivid portrait of Mercy at this time: "It was all quite new then, small, and consequently the student body, faculty and administration were pretty close-knit, and the grand spirit of Sister Mary Etheldreda, President, was felt everywhere...I think the spirit that most marked Mercy in those days was one of closeness and informality. I think it made for an innovative and exciting academic atmosphere."[60]

Although male students had not been "sketched into...[Sister Gratia's] portrait of a College," a male student received permission to take one course at Mercy for teacher certification during the 1966–67 academic year. Sister Etheldreda subsequently initiated a controversial discussion on the possibility of opening Mercy to male students at a September 1968 executive meeting. As part of the follow-up to this meeting, administrators, faculty and students were polled about their feelings on this initiative. The board, which favored the proposal, received the results. Ultimately, it was decided that Mercy should become coeducational, beginning with the 1969–70 academic year to allow time to recruit. To accompany the influx of male students, new "male-oriented" programs, such as pre-law, were added, while others, such as economics and political science, were expanded.[61]

The late 1960s was a difficult financial time for small private liberal arts colleges. Consequently, they welcomed New York State's new multimillion-dollar program to assist private higher-educational institutions. Known as "Bundy aid," the plan developed from a proposal on the future of private

Lay female students enjoy an engaging lecture from a friar. *Mercy College Library Archives.*

A group of female students flee from the College Building (Main Hall) during the early 1960s. *Mercy College Library Archives.*

higher education in New York developed by a committee headed by Ford Foundation president McGeorge Bundy. However, State Education Commission member Edward Nyquist ruled during the 1969–70 academic year, the first year the aid was administered, that numerous colleges were ineligible under the state constitution because of their religious affiliations. Nyquist cited Article XI, Section 3, prohibiting expenditures on "any school or institution of learning wholly or in part under the control or direction of any religious denomination, or in which any denominational tenet or doctrine is taught."[62] In order to obtain Bundy aid, colleges had to be (or become) "independent, non-sectarian" institutions. This condition provoked great debate within the state's Catholic colleges.

Potential access to needed government funds questioned the viability of Mercy's continued formal affiliation with its founders. The Sisters were less concerned about themselves than they were about the College's broader mission and its ability to make the power of education accessible to worthy individuals who might otherwise not have the opportunity. Consequently, the Sisters believed that "the service being provided to the region" by the College was of such "significance and social benefit that it should continue even without the Mercy community's involvement."[63] This hard sacrifice was not easy.

Ultimately, Mercy officially changed its status. In 1969, Sister Etheldreda made appropriate legal notification to New York State, the board chair and the College attorney that "it is the intention of Mercy College to withdraw its Certificate of Religious or Denominational Institution pursuant to Education Law Section 313, if such certification has previously been filed."[64] The College subsequently initiated "steps to loosen up the College's perceived sectarianism." It expanded and diversified its board, changed its regulations regarding Catholic theology courses and deeded the College Building to the College Corporation.[65] As Malcolm Wilson recalled in his 1982 commencement address, "Bundy aid was provided by the State on current degree basis. It was then necessary for the College in order to be eligible for this fund to become an independent college. So the religious oriented college became laicized, and the board was made up mainly of lay men and women."[66]

Not all leaders, including trustees, were completely satisfied with the move toward nonsectarianism and questioned whether changing the College's "label" really changed its character. At the December 12, 1969 board meeting, William Stoutenburgh, shortly before resigning, argued that "it would be well advised to remind anyone inclined to the secularization of this institute, of its origins, purposes, and the role that the Sisters…have played in the funding and development as well as their tremendous contribution both financial and personal, without which Mercy College could never have existed."[67]

From 1969 onward, many of the colleges founded by the Sisters of Mercy either merged with other institutions or closed. During this time, Mercy was unique in that it was the only higher-education institution to which the Sisters relinquished control. Even though many Sisters continued to teach at Mercy, and some served as trustees, the decision to make Mercy independent and nonsectarian marked the beginning of the end of the Sisters' leadership of the institution. The primary concern of those advocating the transition was the College's survival and therefore "an endurance of the spirit of Mercy that animated the place." However, no binding agreement was drafted between the Sisters and the College to guarantee Sister representation on the board. The Sisters did not bargain for any rights, such as tuition reimbursement or affirmative action for Sisters in the hiring process. Further, there was no set agreement for payment for the land and building transferred from the Sisters to the College Corporation, valued in 1978 at $3 million. During the 1970s, the board, chaired by Robert McCooey, and Sister Theresa Kane, province administrator of the Mercy community, worked at resolving these issues.[68]

Moving into the 1970s

As Mercy entered the 1970s, Sister Etheldreda announced her intention to resign as president. Both she and Sister Mary Constance Golden, who had recently resigned as chair of the board of trustees, hoped to rise in the governance structure of the Sisters of Mercy.[69] In May, Sister Frances Mahoney gave a moving testimonial of Sister Etheldreda, noting that she had been with the College "in the growing pains of a maturing institute…in the deliverance of an absolute charter…in the storm and stress of accreditation…[and] in the building of a magnificent library…You found us laymen and laywomen to join us in this great adventure. You worked successfully with Mother Provincial, who supported the concept of contributed services to the College and transferred property and buildings to the College Community." In her early history of Mercy, Sister Agnes noted some of Sister Etheldreda's other successes as president, including expanding student services, enlarging

Sister Mary Etheldreda Christie, whom Dr. Donald Grunewald liked to describe as a "woman for all seasons," during her tenure as Mercy's second president. *Mercy College Library Archives.*

the College facilities and establishing a chapter of the American Association of University Professors (AAUP).

After resigning, Sister Etheldreda became the special assistant to the Commission of Human Rights for New York State (1972–77). She returned to Mercy to serve on its board of trustees and eventually became an administrator in the joint program with Long Island University formed in the 1970s.[70] After Sister Etheldreda, no Sister would again assume the Mercy presidency.

Sister Etheldreda's departure put the board in a difficult position in terms of deciding who would steer the College as it continued to mature as

Dr. Helen (Pat) Coogan, Mercy's first lay president (1970–72), during the late 1960s. *Mercy College Library Archives.*

a nonsectarian institution. In 1970, amid much internal debate, the board appointed Dr. Helen Coogan, chair of the speech department, as College president (and first lay president) on a temporary basis while a search committee looked for a new president. At the end of her tenure in office in 1972, Mercy awarded her an honorary doctorate. Robert McCooey, in expressing the "the sincerity and depth" of the board's gratitude, depicted her as a Renaissance woman and administrator dedicated to "the Mercy tradition of service." He commended her for her "successful stewardship" and noted that she would subsequently return "to her educational love, the classroom."[71] Coogan returned to teaching and developing the Alice Sibernagel Speech and Hearing Center, named in honor of one of Mercy's "dearest former secretaries."[72] Her presidential term marked the transition to a new chapter of Mercy's history. During its "early days of trend setting," Mercy had evolved from a small junior college for Sisters in Tarrytown to a growing, coeducational, accredited four-year institution based in Dobbs Ferry.[73] By the early 1970s, Mercy was well on its way to making its mark as a leader in higher education. But the Sisters left their own lasting mark on the character of the institution.

Chapter 2

BRINGING EDUCATION TO THE PEOPLE, 1972–1990

My passion is to make the good, better and the better, best.
–Dr. Donald Grunewald, Mercy College president (1972–84)[74]

In 1972, a search committee headed by trustee Russell Weiss selected Dr. Donald Grunewald as Mercy's new president.[75] According to Grunewald, he impressed his interviewers by indicating some safety violations he observed during a campus tour to familiarize himself with the College, as well as offering a vision to wed liberal arts education with career-oriented programs. Grunewald (who had completed his DBA at Harvard) had held several high-ranking administrative posts at Suffolk University after leaving his associate professorship at Rutgers. Still in his thirties, he had already authored several books and articles.[76]

At the time, Mercy was a small, struggling, one-campus college with a $2.25 million budget. It had about 1,500 undergraduates, 60 full-time faculty members (with roughly 25 percent holding doctorates), a library of about 60,000 volumes and one building for classrooms and administrative offices. By the end of Grunewald's presidency, it was the eighth-largest private four-year higher-education institution in New York, sprinting on an annual budget of $25 million. It had more than 9,400 undergraduate students, a growing number of graduate students, 230 full-time faculty members (with about 60 percent holding doctorates), a library of more than 385,000 volumes, a home campus with five main buildings, five major extension centers and campuses and a $5 million surplus.[77]

Often noted for his innovative ideas, Grunewald, the expansionist president, and his administration played a large role in defining Mercy's character in its early secular incarnation. Sister Agnes, first chronicler of Mercy's history, described the College's "changing state" during the early 1970s. It needed a new president "who possessed the vision...to build on past accomplishments." In her opinion, Grunewald exceeded all expectations. Reflecting in the 1980s on his presidency, she could only sing his praises:

> *Dr. Donald Grunewald has generously served the Dobbs Ferry Community as an educator, business and civic leader. He has worked tirelessly to keep the Mercy tradition alive and must have "dreamed of things that never were, and said Why not?"...During his exciting years in office, the College has undertaken a new, revolutionary expansion in programs, facilities and administration. Under this fourth President, leadership programs were maintained or enlarged while many new options were introduced...* [T]*he College has changed in many ways during these years of decision making about how best to bring Mercy service to all the Community, and Dr. Grunewald has helped to give the College its image of vitality as well as concern for the underprivileged. Realizing that "life's race is never fully run," he presses on for excellence in education.*[78]

Grunewald's administration was assisted in its efforts by a dedicated and accomplished faculty and board, chaired in succession by Robert McCooey, Frederick Kleisner and Walter Anderson, future editor and CEO of *Parade* magazine and first Mercy male alumnus to serve as a trustee. Grunewald's leadership philosophy allowed administrators wide leeway in establishing and pursuing goals for his or her area jointly with their supervisors, with regular review on their achievements and need for improvement where necessary. With seemingly limitless devotion and energy, he eventually established himself as a respected leader in and around the Mercy community, despite some initial faculty opposition to his appointment due to dissatisfaction with the board's selection process and other issues that created an unsmooth transition to office.[79] The 1975 yearbook, dedicated to Grunewald, praised him for making "both the college and its students the essence of his life," for the "many changes within the College...too numerous to list" and for devoting "all his valuable time to the support of student activities, [where] his attendance is a very regular occurrence."

At the same time, Grunewald made visible appearances locally, joining the boards for nearly a dozen community organizations, social institutions

Dr. Donald Grunewald, Mercy's ambitious and innovative expansionist president (1972–84), shortly after taking office. In a 1984 interview with the *New York Times*, he declared that "being a college president is a lot like the ministry: One has to be called." *Mercy College Library Archives.*

Walter Anderson, Mercy College alumnus and longtime editor of *Parade* magazine, became chairman and CEO of Parade Publications. From 1980 to 1988, he served as chair of the College's board of trustees. *Mercy College Library Archives.*

and educational institutions. As if that were not enough, he also became a member of the Executive Committee of the Council for Small Private Colleges, a fellow of the Institute of Commerce in London, a trustee of Emmanuel College, and a member of the North American Council of the International Association of University Presidents (IAUP).[80]

During the complex transition period immediately before Grunewald's presidency, there had been many administrative changes. Grunewald convinced key former administrators to return as department chairs, with approval of their department faculty, including Dr. Frances Mahoney, chair of the psychology department; Dr. Ann Grow, chair of the philosophy department; and Dr. Coogan, who had built an outstanding speech department. Grunewald retained the acting president's cabinet members and promoted Dr. Gilberto Cancela, who was instrumental in developing an excellent bilingual program, to the cabinet. Some cabinet members, such as Dean of the College Dr. James F. Melville Jr., Director of Admissions Andrew Nelson, Director of Development Anthony A. Ivancich Jr., Executive Assistant Eileen Kappy and Cancela served throughout Grunewald's presidency. From the outset, however, Grunewald and his administration believed that the College required more students to have the financial support needed to increase academic quality, raise inadequate salaries and better serve the students, as well as provide more scholarships for deserving students.[81]

A Growing Institution

During Grunewald's administration, the College launched innovative and aggressive initiatives to expand its student body. As a small, private liberal arts college relying on tuition revenues, Mercy required strong enrollments to maintain its financial health. The alternative, tuition hikes, would contradict Mercy's "mission of access." But "traditional" students (those between the ages of nineteen and twenty-two) became increasingly hard to find as the last baby boomers born after World War II entered college. While still recruiting traditional students, many colleges aggressively competed for "adult," or "nontraditional," students.

Throughout most of the 1970s, Mercy maintained a tuition rate of fifty dollars per credit, the lowest in Westchester, by attracting more students than its competitors. To get these students, Mercy deployed novel marketing strategies derived from the business arena. These strategies included direct mailings, billboards, radio and print advertisements and the use of a recognizable Mercy logo to create a distinct identity program. In fact, Mercy was possibly the first U.S. college to use direct mailings to draw students. Such trailblazing behavior, unorthodox among academic institutions at the time, reflected Grunewald's background and style. The press took note of Mercy's "aggressive marketing and recruiting campaign" and "entrepreneurial approach to education," which rocked "its more established competition."[82] An additional component of this approach was the pioneering use of extension locations throughout the New York metropolitan region.

According to Grunewald, the College's expansion successes, which exceeded his administration's wildest expectations, were the result of happenstance. During the 1970s, problems with the Middle East caused the rationing of gasoline, which limited people's ability to travel. Grunewald's cabinet suggested that Mercy form branch locations closer to potential students for convenience of access. In 1978, Anthony Ivancich expressed this philosophy to the *New York Times*: "We believe that in order to serve the community, it is much better to get to the area where the students are."[83] But finding which locations would attract the most students required trial and error. As Dr. Ann Grow, a key component to the success of Mercy's expansion efforts, later recalled, "If you wanted to experiment you would [first] open an extension site," often located at a local school or community center, before making more significant investments. The "comfortable environment" offered by extension centers helped many achieve higher-educational goals that they might not have otherwise pursued.[84] This approach, which broke from the traditional model of purchasing additional facilities, allowed Mercy to expand more flexibly and cost effectively.

As multiple institutions developed competing extension locations, state officials sought to refine criteria for what constituted an extension site, an extension center and a branch campus based on elements like courses, programs, services and amenities offered at the location.[85] A late 1970s study submitted to the board of regents revealed that Westchester extension centers generally provided substandard educations and were deficient in supervision, facilities, curricular offerings and services. Many also violated state law by granting degrees, a right limited to campuses. At the time, all campus programs needed to be registered with the state for oversight, but extension sites and centers could bypass this procedure. A 1977 meeting between heads of colleges and New York Associate Commissioner for Higher Education T. Edward Hollander had added to the confusion. Hollander urged the creation of a new category between extension sites and branch campuses that would not require the permanence of branch campuses' programs. Consequently, to Grunewald and others, they were carrying out the state's directives. As he informed the press, "We are offering services where the people are and we are fulfilling a real mission laid on us by the state to meet the higher-education needs of the people."[86]

While Mercy was not cited as deficient in the study, the College's name had become synonymous with the extension model, and its competitors depicted the study as a thinly veiled critique of Mercy. Grunewald responded at the time, stating that Mercy offered "quality education at costs that low-to-middle-income people can afford. We consider the faculty, facilities, and curriculum at each of our extension centers equal to, [or]...superior to, those at many other schools." The questioning of academic quality angered Mercy students. As one told the *New York Times*, "I don't think anyone who is serious about obtaining an education would select a school simply because they wanted passing grades. A lot of students who come can't afford to attend schools out of town. I couldn't. But...that doesn't mean that the institution you choose is necessarily lacking in academic standards."[87] In fact, Mercy's academic standards increased during this time.

During Grunewald's administration, Mercy eventually established six major extension centers in New York and Florida. The College began its expansion efforts in 1974 with a center at the Fox Meadow Campus of Northern Westchester BOCES at Yorktown Heights. Its popularity and complexity increased, and in 1976, its library became a federal depository library. Two years later, the center had more than one thousand undergraduates and needed additional space. Mercy negotiated a long-term lease for a two-story building located at the former IBM facility on Strang Boulevard. Both the New York State Education Department and board of regents agreed in October 1978 to change the center's status from an extension center to a branch campus. Consequently, a campus dedication ceremony was held on May 1, 1979. As Grow recalled, becoming a "campus" was "a big deal" at the time. During the early 1980s, Grow, who had successfully helmed Mercy's Bronx Campus, took over the Yorktown Campus. The campus thrived, maintaining a robust campus life, with its own student government, newspaper, journals, clubs and intramural sports. It even launched its own extension programs.[88]

After success in Yorktown, the College offered continuing education programs in 1975 in White Plains to serve the needs of veterans and other adults. The popularity of these programs added traction to the White Plains Center's development. In 1977, a site was selected for the center at the intersection of Martine Avenue and South Broadway. The center increased its cooperation with the Westchester Conservatory of Music, developed a wide assortment of academic offerings and nurtured a growing library

Norman Puffet, who became director of Mercy's first extension center, stands next to the sign for the Yorktown Heights location. *Mercy College Library Archives.*

The pathway from the parking lot to Mercy College's Yorktown Heights Branch Campus. The Campus includes the Washington-Rochambeau Room, which displays works of art. In 1982, the room received a color print, *The Battle of the Cape*, as a gift from local resident Mrs. Samuel H. Ordivay in memory of her husband, a World War II veteran. The room also gained a mural oil painting, courtesy of Florence Bathrick, a secretary at the Yorktown Campus and Mercy alumna. *Photograph by E. Martone.*

that housed the College's paralegal collection.[89] As Michael Mooney, head of the White Plains Center, observed by the end of the decade, the center had "evolved into a dynamic, largely full-service extension center…[It] is a vibrant and dynamic hub of activity with an ideal location in the most cosmopolitan of cities in Westchester." As a result of the White Plains Center's "prosperous growth" during the 1970s, Mooney predicted "a strong run through the '80s." He was correct, as the 1980s witnessed its elevation to a branch campus.[90]

The Bronx Center, which evolved into the Bronx Campus, was also launched in 1975. The center grew quickly at its first location, St. Catharine Academy, where Sister Mary Gratia Maher had once served as principal. In 1977, the Bronx Center was reorganized with Grow as director. As Sister Agnes noted in the 1980s, Grow "added new staff members and built a well-functioning team that has been successful in serving a rapidly growing student population." By 1980, the Bronx Center was servicing more than 1,600 students, offering day, evening and weekend courses. While Grow headed the center, it expanded its physical facilities twice, opened a new library and extended offerings through the PRIDE program for disadvantaged students.[91]

After reviewing multiple potential facilities, Mercy decided in 1976 to open a five-classroom extension center in the Yonkers Cross County Shopping Center. The easily accessible location, affectionately nicknamed the "shopping center college" or the "asphalt campus," became popular, and Mercy had to rent additional space nearby. The Yonkers Center did lack many amenities. But as Alfred Romeo, the center's young "dynamic Director," told the press, the "shopping center ambiance" was a distinct advantage: "It's very appealing to some students. Our cafeteria is a Burger King. The student lounge is the Cross County Pub. The bookstore is the Paperback Booksmith where textbooks as well as current bestsellers can be purchased." The center, because of its location, was regarded in some conservative academic circles as a reflection of "bad taste." However, as Sister Agnes recalled, "Many students found the shopping center to be an easier place to begin or resume college studies" and therefore helped further the College's mission.[92] The Yonkers Center eventually obtained branch campus status in 1986.

Previous, bottom: The side of Mercy College's Yorktown Heights Branch Campus. The Yorktown Campus has thrived into the twenty-first century, remaining Mercy's second-oldest current campus. *Photograph by E. Martone.*

A 1970s photograph of Mercy's extension center in Yonkers. During the mid-1980s, it was elevated to branch campus status. *Mercy College Library Archives.*

In 1976, Mercy also launched its first extension center outside New York. The Miami Center, focusing on bilingual education, opened in Florida under director Dr. Carmen Marina. The center began with two hundred students, mostly Spanish-speaking, with rented space in Miami's "Little Havana." The following year, the center was reorganized with Cancela as dean. While the center copied the courses and syllabi offered at Mercy's New York locations, it developed its own campus life and even held its own commencement exercises. However, the center was short-lived. In 1980, Biscayne College of North Dade, Florida, announced that Mercy's Miami Center would be consolidated into Biscayne as the "Villanueva Center," a name derived from Cuba's Villanueva University.[93]

Amid Mercy's expansion, the College also opened a Peekskill Center. In 1974, representatives of the African American community in Peekskill approached Mercy about establishing a component of the College Opportunity Program in their city. Conditions at that time "were not propitious," but discussions about a Peekskill Center resumed in 1978. City officials offered Mercy space in the new Community Center, located in the Peekskill Field Library Neighborhood Facility, to provide college programs to help "draw adults into the inner city…to demonstrate graphically the rejuvenation of downtown Peekskill." In a 1978 report to the board, Grunewald outlined his vision for the center, explaining that it "offers the first two years of a general liberal arts curriculum, with selected freshman courses in Business and Criminal Justice…[It] is anticipated that those students

Dr. Gilberto Cancela, pictured here, briefly headed Mercy's extension location in Miami, Florida, during the 1970s. *Mercy College Library Archives.*

A 1970s photograph of Mercy's extension center in Peekskill. During the mid-1980s, it was elevated to branch campus status. *Mercy College Library Archives.*

who plan to complete their baccalaureate degree will continue their studies at the Yorktown Campus. Designed primarily for the urban student…the Peekskill Center provides a cosmopolitan business-like atmosphere."[94] In 1986, the Peekskill Center was also elevated to branch campus status.

Meanwhile, the College expanded its main campus into Irvington. In 1974, Mercy pursued the acquisition of the seventeen-acre Allen property. Once part of the Gould estate, the property had become part of the Ardsley Country Club. During the 1960s, investment banker Herbert Allen purchased the end of the club's golf course to build a private mansion overlooking the Hudson. The estate, adjacent to Mercy's campus, included a concrete swimming pool. A picket fence enclosed the area, which then included a double tennis court. The College had made an unsuccessful offer in 1973 to acquire part of the property. The next year, Grunewald and College personnel met with Allen to negotiate the acquisition of the full estate. Allen was then willing to sell the property and even loaned Mercy money to buy it.[95]

Verrazzano Hall, formerly the Irvington property of investment banker Herbert Allen, was added to the Dobbs Ferry Campus during the 1970s. The building's name was determined by a group of prominent Italian Americans that gave the College a large financial gift to establish a Verrazzano Institute of Mediterranean Studies in 1976. *Photograph by E. Martone.*

The Verrazzano Pool was previously part of Herbert Allen's private property. *Photograph by E. Martone.*

Adding the estate to the main campus required a new entranceway. A traffic engineering firm proposed a Hudson Road entrance, with an alternative entrance via Broadway. The board selected the alternative route in 1975. The renovated Allen mansion (now Verrazzano Hall) became home to the president's office, administrative and academic offices and seminar space. Additional parking lots were created on the property, which provided the College community direct access to the Ardsley Railroad Station.[96]

The main campus again expanded when Mercy acquired two additional structures. In 1977, the College purchased the Irvington home of Russell and Polly Beatie on Hudson Road West. The house, "cloaked in a turn of the century peacefulness," included two detached garages and a greenhouse. Dubbed the Social Sciences Building, it was renovated to serve as academic office space. Around the same time, Mercy began renting the house adjacent to the Beatie residence for use as the Professional Studies Building. The College soon purchased this house from Dr. Robert Zimiles, a psychiatrist.[97] A dedication ceremony naming the house in honor of Sister Mary Gratia Maher was held in 1982. Sister Mary Joannes Christie gave a moving tribute to her former colleague, evoking poetry from Blake. As a result of adding these

Dr. Donald Grunewald (center) holds a picture of Sister Mary Gratia Maher during the dedication ceremony of Maher Hall. Standing in the photograph (from left to right) are several College trustees: Sister Gertrude Moran, Lewis Willing, Sister Caroline Laiso, Ann Marie McGowan and Sister Kathleen Ballantine. *Mercy College Library Archives.*

A Mercy College admissions postcard depicting a bird's-eye view of the Dobbs Ferry Campus during the second half of the 1980s. *Mercy College Library Archives.*

properties, the current Dobbs Ferry Campus is no longer predominantly in Dobbs Ferry; more than half of its acreage lies in Irvington. Briefly during the early 1980s, the campus was sporadically referenced in publications as the "Dobbs Ferry/Irvington Campus."[98]

Other changes occurred on the vibrant main campus, which then housed a pub (the Whistle Stop) and a radio station. During the late 1970s, Mercy expanded its athletic programs and developed its athletic facilities on the sloping property behind Main Hall by using landfill. It also developed a tennis court. As Grunewald later recalled, "Some of the trustees were horrified when I added Mercy College's first tennis court in front of the main building so prospective students could see that we had sport facilities." The College immediately opened these facilities to the community. Main Hall received another addition to extend the back of the building, and some administrative offices were relocated to the convent building. Finally, in 1978, the College acquired a house at the corner of Hudson Road and Broadway from actress Julie Harris. For a time, it served as the president's house.[99]

Academic Expansion and Collaboration

As usual, Mercy's students were at the center of its growing academic initiatives. As Grunewald observed in a 1975 report, Mercy "owes a lot to our students who are the heart of the College and who do much to make Mercy such an enjoyable place to work and learn. Their enthusiasm is contagious and their willingness to donate their time and effort to charitable causes in Westchester has done a great deal to enhance the reputation of our College."[100] During Grunewald's administration, Mercy held its first Annual Trustees' Scholarship Dinner and continued to remain a center of intellectual inquiry, hosting local history conferences, lectures on "Genetics and Behavior" and "Bioethical Decision Making and the Public" and a conference on women that focused on the growing interest in women's history and national contributions.[101]

While many liberal arts colleges were struggling amid fierce competition for students, Mercy became a pioneering leader in establishing fruitful consortiums and other collaborations with universities, colleges, community colleges and specialized centers to expand its programs. By pooling resources with other institutions, Mercy provided expansive, innovative programs at lower costs. Consequently, Mercy formed or joined several

MERCY COLLEGE & LIU

ANNOUNCE A NEW

MBA

PROGRAM IN WESTCHESTER

Mercy College and the Brooklyn Center of Long Island University will offer a Masters Program in Business Administration, featuring evening and weekend schedules, quality courses and convenient locations. Courses offered at Mercy College in Dobbs Ferry and Yorktown Heights. Personal interviews available.

For more information call (914) 693-4500, ext. 57 or 74 or write:

Dean of Admissions NYT
Mercy College
555 Broadway
Dobbs Ferry, N.Y. 10522

Please send me more information about your new MBA Program.

Name________
Address________
________ Phone________

A 1975 ad placed in newspapers to promote the collaborative educational efforts of Long Island University and Mercy College. Long Island University eventually established a branch campus at Mercy's Dobbs Ferry Campus that lasted until the late 1990s. *Mercy College Library Archives.*

academic consortiums and signed articulation agreements with area schools and school districts.[102] A particularly long-lasting relationship was formed with the Brooklyn Center of Long Island University (LIU). According to Grunewald, other colleges' opposition, expressed to the state, had thwarted Mercy's efforts to add graduate programs. Consequently, the College sought an alliance with LIU. The Mercy–LIU Brooklyn consortium expanded to include about a dozen programs with shared facilities and administrators. In 1979, the New York Board of Regents authorized the establishment of a branch campus of the Brooklyn Center of LIU at Mercy College. The LIU–Westchester Campus, as it came to be called, ultimately remained at Mercy until 1998.[103]

During this time, the College experimented with new course offerings to appeal to students. For example, Mercy offered African American history courses and, as one newspaper observed in the gender bias typical of the time, courses like "Monsters, Nightmares, and the Occult" and "Women: Myth and Reality" in efforts to "lure housewives out of the department stores during nursery school hours."[104] Rising enrollments allowed the College to add more professors and, in Grunewald's view, expand academic quality. For example, the growing need for English professors to teach the required courses for the growing enrollment meant that the English department could hire additional faculty with different specializations, thus increasing the variety of advanced courses taught by core English professors.

The College developed or expanded groundbreaking programs, like Project AWARE (Adults Who Are Returning to Education) and PRIDE, revived the conferral of associate's degrees and established a Center for Lifelong Learning. The College expanded its undergraduate offerings, especially in career programs. As Grunewald later recalled, "When I came to Mercy, the only major career program for full-time students was a major in education… [W]e converted a part-time evening program in social work into a full-time program and added many new career programs. I wrote the first program in business administration, which became a huge success. The faculty was very kind to its then new president by approving the business major that I proposed despite reservations." Career programs were also added in health sciences. The College's first independent graduate program, in nursing, was launched in the early 1980s despite some protest over increased competition from area colleges and universities with existing nursing programs. Dr. Susan Leddy, Dean Melville and the outstanding nursing and science faculty were among the reasons for the program's success. Meanwhile, Mercy also expanded its prestigious Honors Program, initiated in the early 1970s.[105]

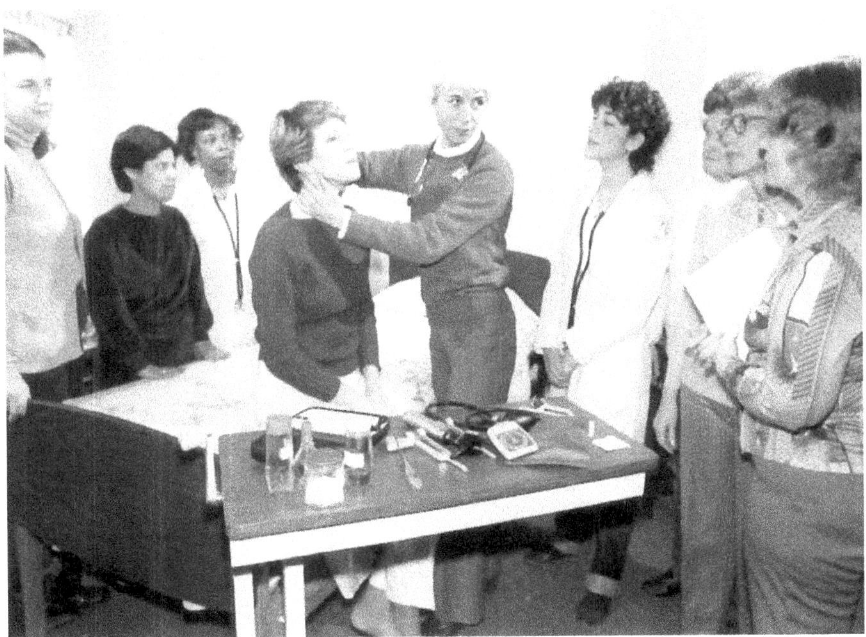

Faculty member Dr. Katie Knight-Perry teaches a nursing class during the 1980s. Mercy College's first independent graduate program, in nursing, was launched during this time. *Mercy College Library Archives.*

Recognizing the benefits of higher education for incarcerated individuals, Mercy developed educational programs for inmates during the mid-1970s. By 1984, Mercy was administering full-time educational programs in more than eleven state correctional facilities. That year, in a letter to the *New York Times*, Professor Thomas Brennan succinctly explained the high social significance of these efforts: "The majority of prison inmates who qualify for the Mercy College programs are highly motivated, extremely hard-working, receptive to learning, ambitious and fully cognizant that a college education is the best guarantee to a decent and firm future in our society…Former convicts with a college education have a better chance at a job than those who lack it, and the educated ex-convict can be one of our better citizens. There are many who already are."[106]

Grunewald's administration also experimented with new ideas to make higher education more convenient for adults. Mercy offered creative (but not always successful) alternative scheduling procedures, including six eight-week sessions instead of traditional spring and fall semesters, evening and weekend courses and even midnight courses! Mercy even had to rent additional space from OLVA. Students enrolling in evening and weekend courses roughly equaled the number of students attending during the day. The increase of evening and "weekend warrior" students created activity at Mercy's main campus during times when it was not so active in the past. These "after hours" students took courses to advance their careers or change their careers or because they needed to work to finance their educational pursuits. As the press noted, "If night school represented access to a better life for immigrants a half century ago, it continues to provide that opportunity today."[107]

To support its academic initiatives, Mercy used national searches to recruit talented new faculty members, provided faculty incentives to obtain doctorates and expanded its library system by acquiring defunct colleges' collections. These acquisitions, coupled with the establishment of branch campus libraries, made the Mercy Library System the second largest among Westchester educational institutions in 1978. During this time, Larry Earl Bone became director of libraries. Under his leadership, the library sought ways to make its total holdings more accessible at extension centers, and with aid from a Kellogg Foundation grant, it participated in a program to develop a computerized online bibliographic system.[108]

By the end of the 1970s, Mercy had clearly become an innovative academic institution. In 1979, during the American Council on Education's annual meeting, Grunewald shared what he perceived as the secrets of

A view of the Dobbs Ferry Campus during the 1980s from the windows of the front entrance to Main Hall. *Mercy College Library Archives.*

Mercy's success in a talk entitled "Growth in Time of Steady State." He cited several factors contributing to Mercy's unprecedented growth. These factors included the recruitment and retention of a strong faculty, the nurturing of a library system, embracing a policy of renting rather than constructing most

A state-of-the-art 1980s computer lab at Mercy College. *Mercy College Library Archives.*

of its expansion facilities, the formation of new programs for career use, the offering of flexible scheduling in terms of both time and location for courses offered, implementing cost-saving programs to keep student costs lower than other private colleges in the region and a student information program that included the direct mailing of 750,000 pieces per year.[109]

The period of intense competition among colleges and universities during the 1970s resulted in a good deal of mudslinging in the media. Mercy's critics at the time often dismissed the College's marketing, academic and expansion initiatives as efforts of a "Mercy Inc." seeking to cash in on nontraditional student markets. Grunewald publicly confronted such unfounded accusations at the time, asking, "What good is having the best mousetrap in the world, if nobody knows about it."[110] He expressed to the press his content with the direction Mercy was heading. "We mail brochures to high schools, employment agencies, and residents at least three times a year," he said. Other schools had already begun to copy Mercy, but Grunewald conceded that he took most of his ideas from colleges located elsewhere. Nevertheless, "We were the first school in Westchester to start an academic consortium, making it possible for us to exchange faculty and students with some of the best schools in the New York area." He expressed his satisfaction at seeing colleges branching out and expanding. "Yes, they may be stepping into Mercy's territory," he declared, "but I welcome competition. In fact, I encourage it!" It was this "just bring it" attitude that had catapulted Mercy to educational excellence.[111]

The crux of critics' accusations against Mercy was that it had betrayed its roots, its altruistic mission set by its foremothers. However, the mission of the nonsectarian, independent Mercy remained fundamentally the same as it had under the Catholic Sisters of Mercy. During the century following the arrival of the Sisters in America, they sought to help women and children who faced social challenges because of class, gender or ethnicity. Often these challenges stemmed from status as "immigrants" and their engagement in unskilled labor. At the time, immigrants had been predominantly of European origin. But in the decades following World War II, the face of America changed. Immigrants from Latin America, the Caribbean and Asia became more prominent.

At the heart of the Mercy mission had been the strong belief that any motivated individual, regardless of class, gender, race, ethnicity or any other social classification, should be provided the opportunity to pursue higher education. Inherent in this belief was the notion that education is power and has the power to transform individuals' lives. By placing access to such power in reach of individuals from groups largely cast outside of elite American society through extension locations, prison programs, consortiums and other means, Mercy took on the role as a harbinger of greater social justice in higher education. It sought to find its "diamonds in the rough," not from among America's rich and powerful, but from among the heart of America, the working class and middle class. Enrolling larger numbers of African American, Latino, Asian and first-generation college students, the College hoped to expand the Mercy mission.

As Grunewald remarked to the press in 1984, "We have an older student population, with an average age of 28. At least one-third of our students come here deficient in language, spoken or written English, and in mathematics. But education has always been the first priority at Mercy. I'm proud of the fact that Mercy has been able to meet the needs of a diverse student population. I'm proud of the fact that many of our students are adults; that they are first-generation college students."[112]

INTERNATIONAL EDUCATION

Grunewald's administration also encouraged initiatives to expand Mercy's international reach that set an ongoing trend for incorporating a global focus to Mercy's curricula. The international initiatives launched at the time ranged from significant developments, like establishing an Institute for the Study of Ethics in 1978 and hosting the Rivertowns Peace Center in 1984, to relatively minor developments, like planting a "peace tree" on the main campus to honor the United Nations' contributions toward global peace during its fiftieth anniversary. In 1979, Mercy held its first All Honor Society Annual Conference, with guest speaker Dr. Robert Mueller, future secretary of the UN's Economic and Social Council and husband of faculty member Dr. Marguerita Mueller. The event helped to increase the College's relationship with UN officials.[113] All these actions brought a new element of academic enrichment to Mercy's programs that reflected changing contemporary trends.

A new generation of American intellectuals emerged following World War II, determined to promote peace, cultural understanding and global connectivity amid an antagonistic Cold War climate. Consequently, Grunewald's administration sought ways to foster international collaboration to benefit Mercy and its students. "By working with our overseas Colleges," Grunewald argued at the time, "our American colleges and universities can help build mutual understanding and help promote peace."[114]

Recognizing the rising economic potential of Asian countries, the College signed "sister institution" agreements with higher-educational institutions in such places as Thailand, Hong Kong, Korea and the Philippines. During the 1970s, through his membership in the IAUP, Grunewald attended multiple international conferences in Asia. During one such meeting in 1979, he visited Thailand as a guest of the king and prime minister and had the pleasant surprise of witnessing Dr. Nibondh Sasidhorn, honorary Mercy degree recipient and head of Srinakarinvrot University, sport a Mercy T-shirt. As a member of IAUP academic delegations, he also toured various East and Southeast Asian academic institutions to evaluate certain academic programs and discuss affiliations and cultural exchanges.[115] As a result of Mercy's growing international reputation, the Costa Rican government invited Grunewald as part of an international academic delegation to visit the country in 1980 to discuss preparations for a conference on a proposed University for Peace. Grunewald also received high marks from national and international institutions for his leadership, receiving honorary doctorates from about half a dozen institutions from around the world.[116]

Another important initiative to further international education was the Verrazzano Institute. During the 1960s, Greenwich Village businessman Gilbert DeLucia nurtured an idea for a contemporary academic institution based on Italian Renaissance culture and values. He chose to name his institution after Giovanni da Verrazzano, the sixteenth-century Italian navigator who explored the Hudson. He and his supporters acquired the former Skidmore College campus at Saratoga, transforming it into "Verrazzano College." Despite opening in 1974 with forty students, it did not have much of a renaissance and closed within a year.

Future New York Supreme Court justice and Italian American community leader Dominic Massaro brought to Grunewald the idea of bringing the concept to Mercy as a semiautonomous institute. Westchester was perceived as an ideal location for such an institute because roughly 40 percent of the county's population at the time was of Italian descent. Further, in 1973, a Dobbs Ferry Historical Society oral history project revealed that 85 percent of the village's center was of Italian descent.[117]

The accepted proposal for a Verrazzano Institute called for "a program of inter-disciplinary studies" to allow students to examine "the Mediterranean culture and the Italian Renaissance not only in terms of their origins but also as they are reflected and interpreted in today's society." The agreements to establish the institute were coordinated to take effect in 1976 on Verrazzano Day (April 17, the day the explorer discovered what is today New York Harbor) and to continue "as long as the Institute's governing board shall fulfill a continuing commitment to ensure its viability as an educational component of Mercy." Its sponsors donated a library collection (about fifty thousand volumes) and $500,000 to name the former Allen mansion after Verrazzano. Several fundraising efforts were also launched throughout the region on the institute's behalf.[118]

Housed in Verrazzano Hall, appropriately overlooking the Hudson, the institute, and its potential for spreading knowledge about Italians' contributions to America, was welcomed by Mercy's many Italian American students. Foreign language professor Dr. Thomas Vesce, who became its director, explained his wish that the institute's offerings would allow students to "understand the Mediterranean values that have formed Western culture, not just for the sake of their own identity…but for a sense of their own potential. I want them to understand the basic Renaissance concept of *vertu*…It means vision…[or] the power to create and to enjoy fully the process of creating." Under the auspices of the institute, students could major in Italian, French or Spanish, combine courses in arts and language or take ethics studies. In the spring 1977 semester, more than fifty students enrolled

Dr. Thomas Vesce, pictured here, was a longtime Mercy faculty member and director of the Verrazzano Institute. *Mercy College Library Archives.*

in the institute, which expanded rapidly and hosted seminars, film festivals, lectures, conferences and journals, remaining a vibrant cultural center at Mercy until 1993.[119]

Shortly after forming, however, the Verrazzano Institute sought affiliations with Mediterranean universities. Mercy became the only American institution authorized to participate in the founding of a new international educational consortium—the Universitas Internationalis Coluccio Salutati, in Pescia, Tuscany. This international university, intended to further international exchanges of students and faculty, was endorsed by the Italian Language Priory of the centuries-old Order of the Knights of St. John of Jerusalem. During the meetings surrounding this initiative, Grunewald and Vesce met many dignitaries in private audiences, including Pope John Paul II. After the pope read a statement in Italian blessing the international university, Vesce and the pope conversed in three languages. The pope asked Grunewald to "convey his blessing and best wishes for the work on the new University to all at Mercy."

While in Italy, Grunewald negotiated proposals with the Pontifical University of St. Thomas Aquinas (the Angelicum) to create various joint programs leading to doctorates. As Grunewald revealed in a memorandum, he hoped "such an affiliation would help Mercy achieve university status without devoting any additional resources…or facilities" since the College "would take advantage of the Angelicum's resources in Rome. It is really a fantastic program." In 1980, Grunewald presented Dr. Michele Martone, prior of the Order of St. John of Jerusalem, Priory of Tuscany, with the President's Medal at a formal observance of the new international university at Verrazzano Hall.[120]

Ending the Early Mercy Era

Meanwhile, the Sisters' direct influence on the College continued to wane. One by one, the members of the order responsible for the College's founding retired. Each retirement was generally greeted with a celebration of the Sisters' contributions to the College. In 1972, for example, Mercy honored Sister Mary Regina Haughney, former Mercy Junior College president and former chair of the College's board of trustees. While granting her an honorary doctorate, the College used the occasion to thank the Sisters as a whole, declaring that "this child, this College wishes to express its debt of gratitude to its greatest benefactor, the Religious Sisters of Mercy and to salute each of these women…[as] the benefactresses of this institution."[121] Three years later, Sister Mary Jeanne Ferrier, former Mercy Junior College president, received an honorary doctorate. During the occasion, she reminisced about her decision to acquire the Gould estate on behalf of her order. In a letter to Robert McCooey, she recalled that "about twenty years ago, I visited this spot for the first time and envisioned the erection of a

Over the years, Mercy College has bestowed honorary degrees on many prominent individuals. In this photograph, Dr. Grunewald presents such an honor to comedian and actor Bob Hope, with aid from Dean Melville and Mrs. Kappy. *Mercy College Library Archives.*

college…[T]he estate at that period was just a forest." It brought her "great joy and happiness" to see what had developed since that time.[122]

In 1977, Sister Mary Etheldreda Christe, Mercy's second president, was the next to receive a long-overdue honorary doctorate. Grunewald had praised her earlier for her "long, untiring, devoted and productive service, for the foundation you built, and for the goals you established." During the ceremony, he thanked her for leaving "upon the College the imprint of your heart and soul."[123] At the end of the 1970s, Mercy honored Sister Mary Stella Roach for her service as trustee, serving through the transition to independent status, with an honorary doctorate. She also became the first "trustee emerita."[124] Finally, in 1981, at an academic convocation celebrating Mercy's twentieth anniversary as a four-year institution, honorary degrees bestowed on members of the faculty teaching since 1961 included several Sisters and former Sisters. The College's decision to continually pay its respects to its founding mothers demonstrated a sense of reverence and appreciation for its past. Within this context, Grunewald encouraged Sister Agnes to compose her history of Mercy "since time and fading memories erode all too soon the fabric of the past."[125]

GRUNEWALD'S DEPARTURE

In 1984, Grunewald, the reputed "educational innovator and entrepreneur," resigned as president. Officially, the decision was based on financial reasons, a desire to spend more time with his family (he married while president and now had a young family), a wish to focus on publishing and a desire to return to teaching. In a *New York Times* article, Grunewald revealed, "I had accomplished much of what I wanted to do. I think it's healthy for both the institution and the individual to do different things at different times. Over the years, one becomes less effective and a new face can do better. You see it in politics." His only unrealized dream for Mercy, he declared at the time, was its attainment of university status. But, he noted, "others did not share my vision." In Mercy's annual report, Walter Anderson echoed these sentiments.[126] In retrospect, Grunewald elaborated on what he perceived as his failures, including an attempt to start a Mercy law school. "We lost out to Pace," he revealed, "which had been working on such a proposed law school for some years." He was also unsuccessful in obtaining the state's permission to launch a doctoral program in psychology due to oppositional lobbying to the state from other colleges and universities unhappy with Mercy's successful expansion to the Bronx.[127]

However, toward the end of his term, Grunewald's difficulties with the board also multiplied. He received increased criticism over his rapid and extensive expansion initiatives and their consequences, particularly the move to Miami. A Middle States evaluation team cautioned against continued rapid expansion, suggesting that it was perhaps too much too soon and offering concern over the maintaining of academic quality that ultimately resulted in the creation of the post of provost. The board was also interested in expanding Mercy as a national, rather than local, institution. Grunewald remained at Mercy for two more years as a distinguished professor and briefly became president and CEO of the Hudson River Museum.[128] He subsequently became a professor at Iona College.

Before exiting, however, Grunewald gave some advice for his successor as president, a post he described lightheartedly to the press as "a professional beggar." He joked to the *New York Times* that his successor should make sure that he or she had the "stomach of a goat" because of the many lunches and dinners associated with the president's duties. On a serious note, he declared that the job required dedication and hard work, for "a lot of time is spent on fund raising, whether it's going after donors from corporations or grants from Government or finding new ways to bring students." He regarded the Mercy mission as immutable and noted that future presidents should possess a healthy respect for it, for "no matter what becomes of our institution, I see Mercy having the same mission…a mission to serve all communities."[129]

Looking back at his time as president, Grunewald noted his many accomplishments, including unparalleled increases in enrollment, the improvement of academic quality, reaccreditation, the development of new facilities, the launching of five major branch centers and campuses and the buildup of financial surpluses and endowment. Further, President Gerald Ford and the Academy for Educational Development cited Mercy as one of the most innovative colleges in the United States during Grunewald's leadership in recognition of its growth in academic quality and service to its students.[130]

One of Grunewald's overlooked legacies to the College was the tradition of commissioning portraits of Mercy's presidents and chairs displayed in the Rotunda. His portrait and others were painted by local artist Alton Tobey, who also painted *Roots of Westchester*, a mural in the Westchester County Courthouse. While creating the mural, Tobey incorporated more than one hundred individual portraits, from George Washington to then contemporary county residents, into his composition. Grunewald and Anderson are among those included.[131]

GROWING PAINS AND THE DIPLOMAT: DR. WILBERT LEMELLE AND THE LATE 1980s

While the board searched for a successor during the 1984–85 academic year, Dr. Merle Kling served as interim president, a position that then paid a $64,000 annual salary. Kling had spent most of his career as a political science professor and administrator at Washington University in St. Louis. In the early 1980s, he had just retired from his post as provost and executive vice-chancellor.[132] According to Grow, Kling was a "wise, mature leader." Mercy could have benefitted from his prolonged leadership, she believes, but he was only in the area for a temporary period of time.[133]

The board, interested in selecting a sixth president with a diverse background, ultimately selected Dr. Wilbert J. LeMelle, Mercy's first African American president. Competent in seven foreign languages, he was born in New Iberia, Louisiana. After leaving the seminary and earning his doctorate in international relations at the University of Denver, LeMelle embarked on a distinguished career, working for the Ford Foundation (1964–77), serving as U.S. ambassador to Kenya and Seychelles during the Carter administration and working as associate vice-chancellor of the State University of New

A banner announcing the inauguration of Mercy College's sixth president, Dr. Wilbert J. LeMelle, in 1985. *Mercy College Library Archives.*

York system. He became such a prominent intellectual that his hometown honored him with an "Ambassador LeMelle Street."[134]

Upon accepting his new position at Mercy, LeMelle confided to the press that he had no clear plans. "What I hope to do in the next few months," he revealed, "is learn as much as I can about the Mercy tradition." He did, however, note that he had "some ideas" centering on his passion for international education and language study that would affect his actions. He hoped that Mercy could offer increased international programs, which he felt were not receiving proper funding during the Reagan era. "I think it's a great tragedy and we are the losers as a people by this deterioration of our knowledge of the wider world," he told the *New York Times*. LeMelle felt strongly about the need to learn about other cultures, civilizations and global politics "in order to avoid some of the potential conflicts that will arise out of ignorance." He also expressed a hope to enlarge Mercy's international student body. LeMelle believed that running Mercy would pose no overwhelming or unusual challenges, citing his experiences at the Ford Foundation as providing him "with some understanding of the issues."[135]

During his presidency, LeMelle developed many ambitious plans for the College and had several accomplishments, including some academic reforms, like the revision of the general education curriculum, enhanced coordination and funding of student support services, the establishment of writing centers and a math lab and the development of a program for students with learning disabilities. He fostered a revitalized marketing campaign, reorganized the admissions office and launched the first phase of an international studies program through a President's Lecture Series that brought ambassadors to Mercy.[136] Mercy also purchased and renovated a facility at Antin Place to house its growing Bronx Campus. At the time, this was one of the only College-owned facilities other than the main campus.

During this time, as a result of generous donations from faculty member Dr. Marie McKellar and her husband in honor of her parents, Mercy gained the Bernard Hank Software Laboratory and the Viola Hank Mathematics Laboratory and Computer Classroom.[137] Nevertheless, the late 1980s "appear in Mercy lore as the nadir of the College's history," primarily because enrollments had taken a nose dive to barely five thousand students by 1990, hurling the College into "crisis mode." The Yonkers Campus closed in 1989 to reduce costs (although Mercy would continue to operate other sites there), salaries were frozen and faculty was downsized.[138]

A strange case also developed around Mercy's most famous "non-alumnus." A large scandal emerged when Victor Botnick, a top aide to New

The ribbon-cutting ceremony for the Bronx Branch Campus at Antin Place. *From left to right*: Dominic Massaro, New York Supreme Court justice; Gerald Weinbrecht, director of the Bronx Campus; William Rose Jr., chair of the board of trustees; President LeMelle; and Fernando Ferrer, Bronx Borough president. *Mercy College Library Archives.*

Mercy's Bronx Branch Campus at Antin Place. *Mercy College Library Archives.*

York City mayor Ed Koch and chairman of the city's Health and Hospitals Corporation, was found to have fabricated his requirements for his position by falsely claiming a prestigious Mercy degree.[139]

Meanwhile, the Sisters' declining membership, along with other factors, encouraged them in the late 1980s to sell nearly sixty acres of Mount Mercy property, including the Wickers Creek area, for the construction of what became the Landing at Dobbs Ferry, a townhouse development. The building of the development on the L-shaped land parcel fronting the Hudson was delayed through the 1990s due to builder difficulties and environmental and archaeological concerns.[140] This property, which Mercy had considered an unofficial part of its campus, included Mercy Beach, a graveyard and the Sisters' former provincialate (Christie Hall). The College had used Christie Hall (named in honor of Sisters Mary Joannes and Mary Etheldreda Christie) for office space and other needs. "An emotional resource" tied to Mercy's early history, the building was demolished after the sale, creating "a strain of the collective psyche" of the College community.[141]

In his president reports, LeMelle acknowledged the "pressure of declining enrollments" on revenues and Mercy's growing deficit. He perceived the most

Christie Hall, named in honor of founding faculty members (and biological sisters) Sister Mary Etheldreda Christie and Sister Joannes Christie, was demolished in the 1980s to make room for a townhouse development that eventually became the Landing at Dobbs Ferry. *Mercy College Library Archives.*

important challenge as enrollment management. He reported "aggressive" recruiting efforts and appointed an acting dean for admissions, and the provost's office assumed greater supervision of finances to reduce costs while maintaining the Mercy mission. Some of Mercy's problems at the time stemmed from the negative consequences of its rapid and continued expansion that had begun to materialize during the end of Grunewald's administration. Other problems stemmed from social and economic changes unfolding during the 1980s. Consequently, while many of the College's difficulties at the time were not a direct result of LeMelle's actions, he ultimately received the blame for Mercy's temporarily sagging fortunes. He decided to resign as president in 1990.[142]

Despite the brief period of growing pains during the late 1980s, the period between 1972 and 1990 was one of great progress for Mercy. As the 1983 Middle States Periodic Review explained, the College had evolved "from a small, progressive, liberal arts college for women into an independent, non-sectarian, coeducational, multi-campus institution enrolling more than 9,000 students, from all age groups, who represent the cultural, racial, religious, social and economic diversity of the New York metropolitan area...All this is done at tuition levels lower than most other independent colleges and universities in the immediate geographic area."[143] The College continued to thrive and build on the changes made during this period as Mercy entered the 1990s and a new millennium.

Chapter 3

The Race to the Top, 1990–2013

Mercy, having attained full maturity, will add glowing chapters to education in America.

–Sister Mary Joannes Christie, Mercy College founding faculty member[144]

In 1990, Mercy's new seventh president, Dr. Jay Sexter, former provost and vice-president for academic affairs at John Jay College, focused on returning Mercy to prominence. Sexter, described in the press as possessing a "penchant for the nitty-gritty of the business world," had been famously dubbed "the professor who brings home the bacon" in a 1977 *Forbes* article. He now faced what was described at the time as the "formidable challenge" of increasing Mercy's enrollments and reducing its deficit. Despite facing some criticisms along the way, Sexter helped put the College on a path that generally resulted in stable growth during the 1990s, leading a "return to Mercy's traditions of innovation and outreach." Working in conjunction with a strong board, an excellent faculty and staff and a dedicated student body, Mercy began its inevitable rise to the top as an academic leader in higher education.[145]

The Sexter Years, 1990–99

Early in his administration, Sexter capitalized on the connections he had forged with local school districts to open new extension sites in Westchester and New York City. These efforts echoed Grunewald's administration's rapid expansion initiatives during the 1970s. By 1993, these extension sites had enrolled more than one thousand students, and the College's already diverse student population, a hallmark of its thriving campus life, became even more diversified, as new extension locations blossomed in areas heavily populated with new immigrants (especially from Asia, Latin America and eastern Europe) and underrepresented minorities.

However, the proliferation of new and expanded extension sites and centers revived some of the former administrative problems of the 1970s and 1980s. In 1994, the Middle States Association cautioned against renewed, rapid expansion. Consequently, the College halted its expansion initiatives and gradually reduced the number of its extension sites.[146] During this time, for example, Mercy relinquished its Peekskill Campus to Westchester Community College. In 1996, Mercy reorganized the governance of its extension centers after Dr. Ann Grow resigned as vice-president for extension centers. The reorganization included future Mercy president Dr. Louise Feroe's promotion to assistant vice-president for academic affairs. She had come to Mercy as a faculty member during the 1980s.[147]

During President Sexter's administration, Mercy College began to resume its expansionist endeavors. During the early 1990s, the College had more than a dozen active extension locations, including this one in Mount Vernon. *Mercy College Library Archives.*

While some extension sites, centers and campuses faced closure, others were booming. The Bronx Campus reached and exceeded its capacity, and the College expanded its presence in Manhattan. In 1993, the College considered purchasing the Center for Media Arts. Students attending the center had the option to apply their courses toward a degree at Mercy, while the center's acquisition would have added fully equipped television and radio studios to Mercy's facilities. Shortly thereafter, Mercy opened a new branch campus in Manhattan at St. Michael Academy. In an interview, former Mercy president Dr. Donald Grunewald praised Sexter's accomplishments, especially the establishment of a branch campus in Manhattan, which was something he had wanted to do but failed to achieve.[148]

During the 1990s, Mercy continued to be a tuition-driven institution and relied on strong enrollments to maintain a healthy financial state. As part of its vigorous efforts to recruit traditional and older, nontraditional students, Mercy initiated some unorthodox recruitment efforts. In 1995, for example, the College developed "an audacious incentive system" receiving wide media coverage that tied faculty salaries to enrollment levels. If professors' recruitment efforts resulted in a set enrollment increase, they would receive a 7 percent salary increase; otherwise, they would receive a reduction. An "enthusiastic" faculty increased enrollment by 20 percent.[149]

Sexter's administration introduced enrollment incentive programs, including tuition discounts for extension sites and a 50 percent tuition discount for individuals receiving unemployment benefits to make it easier for people who had lost their jobs to gain training for career changes. Mercy's flat-rate tuition plan, introduced in the mid-1990s amid cuts in New York State aid, was revolutionary for its time. Because of reduced aid, many colleges cut programs and increased tuition. However, as Sexter remarked to the press, the "[Chinese] symbol for a problem is the same as for an opportunity." He chose the opposite path of other colleges, reducing Mercy's tuition rates by allowing full-time students to pay a flat fee per semester rather than pay by individual credits. The plan, which saved students 7 percent tuition costs and encouraged them to complete their degrees promptly, was designed to make Mercy stand out from its competitors and create a surge in enrollments. Throughout the decade, tuition revenue steadily increased with better enrollments, and the College improved its revenue totals from government sources. By 1998, Mercy even had a modest surplus of $3.5 million.[150]

Efforts to improve Mercy's financial state were accompanied by efforts to improve its academic offerings. While enrollment at most local colleges dropped or stagnated, Mercy used innovative and diverse offerings to attract students. Consequently, Mercy's enrollment, about 4,800 students in 1990, rose to about 7,000 in 1994. Some of these groundbreaking offerings included a Korean bilingual program, efforts to welcome Spanish-speaking students and the creation of the Institute for the Study of English to help immigrants learn English.[151] Some long-standing Mercy programs, however, were cut due to the reduction or elimination of funding. For example, Mercy regretfully ended its programs for prison inmates in the mid-1990s following the elimination of government funding for such initiatives. However, the College soon revived its commitment to bring higher education to incarcerated individuals, working with private organizations such as the nonprofit Hudson Link for Higher Education.[152]

By the 1990s, student retention rates had become an issue of national concern. At the forefront of trends in higher education, Mercy launched studies to examine its own retention patterns to develop new initiatives for improvement. The College strengthened its student support services, established campus Learning Centers, introduced freshman clusters and developed competency requirements for students in fundamental skills expected of college graduates. Mercy also acquired the Sisters' remaining property on the Dobbs Ferry Campus, primarily for creating student dorms, which were opened in the mid-1990s, to attract students from beyond the local region. In addition, Mercy revised its technological infrastructure and outsourced computer service management.[153]

One of the most significant academic successes of Sexter's administration was the expansion of Mercy graduate programs, primarily in 1995 and from 1998 to 1999. After dissolving its long-standing partnership with LIU in the late 1990s, Mercy quickly registered a flurry of graduate programs with the state under its own name. Sexter's success in this endeavor was possibly aided by the reputation of Mercy's graduate program in nursing and the fact that so many faculty members from Mercy taught in the LIU-Westchester graduate programs with great accomplishment. By 2006, graduate students composed 38 percent of Mercy's total enrollment, a dramatic increase from the 3 percent that they had composed only a decade previously. The College devoted resources to support its graduate programs to make them a success, including the establishment of a Graduate Center at Dobbs Ferry and the administrative post of graduate dean.[154] Mercy continued its commitment to educate first-generation college students and ranked among the top universities conferring degrees to African American and Hispanic students. The College developed a unique acupuncture program, worked with the Westchester Teaching

Dr. Jay Sexter, dubbed "the professor who brings home the bacon" in a 1977 *Forbes* article, served as Mercy's seventh president from 1990 to 1999. In this photograph, Sexter, standing to the left, poses next to the College's new electronic sign (and Pepsi advertisement) located at the entrance of the Dobbs Ferry Campus. *Mercy College Library Archives.*

Academy to get teachers certified and offered the only graduate programs in physical therapy and occupational therapy in Westchester. According to Grunewald, Sexter privately reached out to his predecessor to consult with him on the development of these latter programs in the health science areas. In addition, Mercy developed and expanded its online course offerings.[155]

During the 1990s, several notable changes also occurred among the College's senior administration. Dr. Carol Moore, for example, became provost in 1992, replacing Dr. Peter French. She helped strengthen strategic planning, developed a process for regular program reviews, enhanced faculty assessment and raised standards for tenure and promotion. Shortly after Sexter became president, William A. Rose Jr. resigned as chair of the board of trustees. Alumna Wanda Borges took over the position until the mid-1990s, when she was succeeded as chair by Francis Ronnenberg. At about the same time, Sister Agnes O'Grady resigned as trustee, ending the Sisters' presence on the board. However, she expressed in a 1997 interview her content that "the Mercy mission was still explicitly a benchmark for board actions."[156]

During the 1990s, despite the Sexter administration's successes, a "contentious atmosphere" developed between faculty and staff with senior administration. Some staff members even unionized in response. The existing AAUP chapter, however, failed to enroll more than 50 percent of the faculty as dues-paying members. Faculty discontent rose during the search for Sexter's replacement after he announced his intention to resign in 1997. The board selected a candidate whom faculty perceived as unqualified. The board and the faculty, which questioned the search process, worked to resolve the matter. The candidate eventually withdrew, and the board asked Sexter to remain president until 1999 to enable a new search. A search conducted by a professional firm resulted in Dr. Lucie Lapovsky's appointment as Mercy's eighth president.[157]

ENTERING A NEW MILLENNIUM: PRESIDENTS LAPOVSKY AND FEROE, 1999–2008

Dr. Lucie Lapovsky, an economist and former chief financial officer at Goucher College, had recently been listed by the *Daily Record* of Maryland as among the state's top one hundred women. In an interview for an article on her appointment as Mercy's eighth president, she discussed her unique paperweight collection, which served as the inspiration for her vision for Mercy. She remarked, "I want them close by...They encourage me to keep dreaming." Among these dreams was the hope to give "students a helping hand in the world." Lapovsky perceived her mission as helping Mercy's students realize their full potential, to become the "jewels" of society.[158]

As usual, academics remained a priority at Mercy. Lapovsky's administration launched efforts to strengthen the general education curriculum, raised standards for academic support services and increased the number of core faculty. Retention improvement continued to be a main concern. The College upgraded its admission standards to select better-prepared students more likely to follow through to graduation and more than doubled the graduation rates of students. Mercy's commitment to developing innovative programs to provide opportunities for motivated students continued.

The College maintained its ranking among the top colleges and universities conferring degrees to Hispanic and African American students. It also developed the region's first graduate program in Internet business systems and launched academic initiatives in response to local needs.[159] For example, New York State created a potential teacher shortage crisis when it stopped issuing temporary certification for certain teaching positions. This decision threatened not only several teachers' job security but also school districts' ability to adequately staff schools. To help avert this crisis, Mercy developed an alternative, highly flexible certification program in cooperation with New York City school districts to meet their needs while addressing the state's standards. With Americorps sponsorship, the graduate-level Individualized Certification Plan for Teachers (ICPT) quickly flourished under Dr. Esther Wermuth's leadership. Mercy also received a $1.14 million grant from the U.S. Education Department to develop an alternative teacher certification program (HEADS-UP) benefiting Bronx schools.[160]

During the early 2000s, Mercy used its better financial position to support new and upgraded facilities and to enhance student, faculty and staff support. Consequently, the College upgraded and expanded its facilities at Dobbs Ferry, renovating its biology labs, building a new Speech and Hearing Center, remodeling the cafeteria, expanding the student and faculty lounges and developing a new Learning Center. As Mercy greeted the new millennium, it suffered the loss of Dr. Frances T.M. Mahoney, who had joined Mercy during the 1960s as Sister Maureen. During her more than forty devoted years of service, she had served as a member of the College's faculty, administration and trustees. Shortly before she passed away, Lapovsky had informed her of the board's decision to honor her by naming the Social Sciences Building "Mahoney Hall." In addition to the changes on the main campus, Mercy made technology upgrades, launched a website, developed an intranet site and began to make student services available online. The College even temporarily supported a new radio station. After increasing the standards for facilities and services at extension locations, the College reduced or eliminated the tuition discounts that had characterized the Sexter era.[161]

Lapovsky's administration also launched bold initiatives for Mercy's White Plains, Manhattan and Bronx Campuses. Extra space was added to the White Plains Campus, which was reconfigured to include high-end digital studios, an art studio, an auditorium, a new cafeteria and a student lounge. The White Plains Campus nurtured programs in computer graphics, digital animation, website design and related subjects.[162] The heart of the campus became its Center for Digital Arts, which included professional-level sound recording studios, high-end computer labs and an art studio. The campus also came to include the Mortimer Levitt Auditorium, named in honor of the philanthropist founder and president of the Custom Shop.

Dr. Frances T.M. Mahoney, who began her career at Mercy College in 1960 as Sister Maureen, was a beloved and dedicated member of the College community. During her decades of service, she occupied various faculty and administrative roles. During Dr. Lucie Lapovsky's administration, the College decided to name the Social Sciences Building "Mahoney Hall" in her honor. *Photograph by E. Martone.*

Meanwhile, the Manhattan Campus transferred from St. Michael Academy to a grand home at Herald Square. St. Michael Academy, which opened in 1874, closed in 2010 shortly after the transfer. The new, state-of-the-art Manhattan Campus soon received a distinguished visitor, First Lady Laura Bush, in 2003. She visited Mercy to draw attention to the College's role in training teaching fellows. The Manhattan Campus, which includes the spectacular Roy Disney Center for Animation, has brought a cosmopolitan flair to Mercy and an even greater presence in the New York metropolitan area.[163]

Finally, during the 1990s, Bronx enrollments surged, with the number of students exceeding the existing facility's capacity. In January 2004, Mercy opened a new, state-of-the-art Bronx Campus at the Hutchinson Metro Center, an office complex built by the Westchester-based Simone Development Company during 2002–3 over the former site of the Bronx Developmental Center, a 1970s state mental health facility designed by

Mercy College's Manhattan Campus. *Mercy College Library Archives.*

The new state-of-the-art Bronx Branch Campus, housed in the Hutchinson Metro Center, opened in 2004. *Mercy College Library Archives.*

renowned architect Richard Meier and noted for its "space-age design." The Bronx Campus boasts a landscaped courtyard, dining areas, the French Family Auditorium, the Marsha and James McCormick Library, an atrium named in honor of community leader Naomi Rivera, wired classrooms, substantial student support space, science labs, a behavioral science research lab and several computer labs.[164]

Mercy's distance learning programs also expanded. The momentum for distance learning at Mercy had begun during the late 1980s as an "outgrowth of faculty interest in new teaching methodologies." In 1990, Dr. Frank McCluskey, a philosophy professor, received an IBM grant to develop Mercy's online learning program. The College quickly became a "pioneer in the online learning environment." Mercy's online and hybrid courses, eventually offered through the Mercy Long-distance Instructional Network (MerLIN), continued to expand, and the College became one of largest online educational providers in New York. By the early twenty-first century, Mercy's online learning community had grown substantially.[165]As an official report declared in 2003, "We now consider the Online Campus, led by a Dean of Online Learning, to be the sixth Mercy Campus." The proliferation of home computers and the flexibility of asynchronous online learning made the increased use of extension centers and creative scheduling less necessary for Mercy's mission of access. Because of this reason, and many other factors, the College began to reduce and consolidate its extension locations. By the end of 2003, the College was operating only four extension sites and centers (down from a high of thirteen during the mid-1990s) in addition to its branch campuses in Yorktown, White Plains, the Bronx and Manhattan. Lapovsky's administration also dismantled the Office of Extension Centers and opened no new extension locations, although the Yonkers site was relocated to another location in Yonkers.[166]

Changes also occurred at the senior administrative level during Lapovsky's tenure as president. For example, Dr. Louise Feroe, who had become acting provost in 1998, became provost in 1999. The new administration sought to reevaluate the College's strategies, objectives and operating procedures and held retreats and monthly meetings. In addition, Lapovsky's administration sought to enhance existing community relations and the amount of donations and grants from private foundations. According to Dr. Ann Grow, Lapovsky had a "talent for raising money." During her administration, an expanded board became more active with donations and raising funds for the College. For example, Edward Dunn, chair of the board of trustees for Lapovsky's tenure as president, undertook major fundraising initiatives and made generous financial contributions. His service to the College led to the development of the current Center for Student Success and Engagement being named in his honor. Former chair Francis Ronnenberg and his wife, Mary Ellen, became founders of the Ronnenberg Legacy Society, which recognizes alumni, faculty, staff and supporters who make munificent commitments to Mercy through estate and planned giving. However, amid the development of new campuses in the Bronx and Manhattan and the reorganization of Mercy's financial infrastructure, the College had a deficit in 2002.[167] Lapovsky eventually stepped down as president in 2004. The board appointed Feroe as interim president for two years before appointing her president.

During Feroe's administration, Mercy continued to attract national attention for its academic programs. For example, it received national recognition for welcoming Hispanic students and was among the twenty institutions selected nationwide to participate in the Teachers for the 21st Century program, designed by the Council of Independent Colleges with financial support from Microsoft. The College became the first in New York, and possibly the first in the United States, to offer a business degree in corporate and homeland security. Mercy also offered its first doctoral degree

Four Mercy College presidents. *From left to right*: Dr. Donald Grunewald, Dr. Louise Feroe, Dr. Jay Sexter and Dr. Lucie Lapovsky. *Mercy College, Public Relations.*

program (physical therapy) in 2007 and conferred its first doctoral degrees in 2008.[168]

Mercy also continued to make changes to better support its students and campus life. For example, the College launched efforts to develop a "one-stop student services concept" to offer students "the utmost in convenience and customer service." Bruce Fulton, who became director of libraries in 2000, shifted the library system's focus toward the accumulation of electronic materials and database subscriptions to more closely align with research trends in the digital age. Mercy also developed a long-term IT strategy. In addition, Mercy developed a new mascot and nickname. The "Mercy Flyers" had used an eagle as a mascot, but its use had been phased out by the early 2000s. In 2007, the College unveiled the new "Mavericks" nickname and mascot.[169]

Feroe's administration, which helped stabilize the College's financial position, also included several personnel changes and restructuring efforts to streamline operations. In 2007, Mercy welcomed several new members to its senior administrative team, including its first chief operating officer, its first chief compliance officer and general counsel, a new provost and a new vice-president for institutional advancement.[170] The new leadership team brought a revitalizing energy to the College's upper ranks. However, in 2008, Feroe stepped down as president and became a senior administrator in the Connecticut State University System until 2012.

Achieving National Excellence: President Kimberly Cline, 2008 to the Present

Mercy needed a new president who could balance a vision for the College's future that not only adapted it to the changing times while remaining faithful to its founders' vision but also maintained an eye on the bottom line. In 2008, the board selected Dr. Kimberly R. Cline as Mercy's tenth president. Cline, who grew up in North Carolina and earned her degrees from the University of North Carolina–Chapel Hill and Hofstra University, already had extensive and impressive educational administrative experience. She had served previously as vice-chancellor and chief financial officer of the State University of New York System. As she once remarked to the press about the experience, "I was able to see sixty-four college presidents in action…It was like benchmark training by osmosis."[171] She had also held positions at SUNY, Maritime College (vice-president, chief operating officer and chief of staff), Seton Hall (vice-president for finance

Dr. Kimberly Cline began her tenure as Mercy College's tenth president in 2008. During her time as president, the College's national reputation has soared largely because of its revolutionary PACT program, dedication to student success, high-quality and affordable programs and commitment to innovation in education. *Mercy College, Public Relations.*

and administration) and Hofstra University (university attorney, assistant treasurer, assistant vice-president for business affairs and School of Business faculty member).

Upon making the announcement regarding Cline's appointment, Richard E. French Jr., board chair, proudly remarked, "Dr. Cline's achievements make her the right president to lead Mercy College. I am confident she will work collaboratively with the faculty, staff, and students to enhance the stature of Mercy College." Before assuming the presidency, Cline demonstrated her work ethic and enthusiasm for her new post, eagerly learning about the College and making visits to several local schools and community colleges to establish rapport and launch recruitment efforts. She perceived her administration's mission as reinforcing Mercy as a student-centered learning institution by "creating a culture of caring, giving the students a good experience and readiness for life" and by creating "a sense of family on campus."[172]

TABLE 2. PRESIDENTS OF MERCY COLLEGE, 1961–PRESENT

Sr. Mary Gratia Maher	1961–1962
Sr. Mary Etheldreda Christie	1962–1970
Dr. Helen Coogan	1970–1972
Dr. Donald Grunewald	1972–1984
Dr. Merle Kling	1984–1985
Dr. Wilbert J. LeMelle	1985–1990
Dr. Jay Sexter	1990–1999
Dr. Lucie Lapovsky	1999–2004
Dr. Louise H. Feroe	2004–2008
Dr. Kimberly R. Cline	2008–

Cline, dubbed "the experimenter" in a *Westchester Magazine* article, was appointed to the board of the Commission on Independent Colleges and Universities shortly after becoming president and quickly demonstrated "strong, visionary leadership" that made a major impact on the College.[173] With roughly half of students nationwide finishing their degree programs, low retention and completion rates had reached crisis levels, especially among low-income, minority and first-generation students. For some time, Mercy had been exploring its own retention patterns and ways to improve retention rates, with mixed results.

Under Cline's new leadership, Mercy developed a new program with federal funding to address this problem. The Personalized Achievement Contract (PACT) program sought to create a "one-stop shop" for students to get help in resolving any problems from an assigned mentor, as well as to encourage their academic growth and development. The program provides each student with a mentor cross-trained in various services to act as his or her go-to source for help with any problem. Mentors begin by contacting accepted students and their families, then assist with application and financial aid processes, housing and so on, giving each student individual attention to help him or her make a smooth transition to college, through college and to the "real world." Each mentor also works proactively with the student to set and follow up on goals, explore career options and internship possibilities and find leadership opportunities. PACT, therefore, reverses the trend of increasing student anonymity, common in large colleges and universities, as individual students become lost within large student bodies and a bureaucracy lacking customer service skills.

While PACT ultimately sought to improve student retention rates, at its core was a commitment to student achievement and personal growth. As Cline revealed in an interview, "We are helping them maximize their potential. We're not just helping them get through college and get a job…We try to focus on helping our students find the career choices that will give them lifetime success." Mercy piloted the program with fifty students during the spring 2009 semester. The College steadily increased the number of students involved with the program, with the goal of including all students. PACT attracted much national attention as a potential national model to meet retention and completion challenges. In 2009, the National Association of Colleges and Employers named PACT a "Best Practice" for retention and career services. As a result of PACT's success, Mercy received further federal funding to extend PACT as an option to graduate students. Cline quickly perceived the innovative program as the cornerstone of Mercy's national reputation. PACT is continually cited as a core reason for the College's transformation and its students' successful outcomes. This revolutionary mentoring program directly addresses the national agenda to raise the number of college graduates in America to the highest in the world by 2020.[174]

During the 1970s, Dolores Del Bello, director of External Affairs, helped develop a new identity program for Mercy College. Part of this program included the College's "blue max" logo, which became a long-recognized emblem of Mercy College. As the College embarked on a bold new path toward increased academic excellence during the new millennium, it embraced a stylish new logo. In this picture, depicting a balance between Mercy College's past and present, a banner bearing the College's new logo flies near a sculpture depicting the former "blue max" emblem. *Photograph by E. Martone.*

PACT, however, was not Mercy's only visionary initiative designed to maximize student success. The College partnered with the KIPP Foundation, the umbrella nonprofit organization for a national network of public charter schools, to improve college completion rates across the country, especially for young people from low-income communities. In 2011, Mercy also launched Kaleidoscope, a program to help reduce educational costs and improve student outcomes using Open Educational Resources (OER).

The College launched many new academic initiatives and consolidated its existing academic offerings. In 2008, Mercy adopted a new organizational structure, replacing its previous eight divisions with five schools: Business, Education, Health and Natural Sciences, Liberal Arts and Social and Behavioral Sciences. By the 2000s, Mercy was offering more than ninety undergraduate and graduate programs and maintaining a vibrant online learning community, using Blackboard software, that brings higher education to anyone, anywhere, at any time. The College continued to emphasize its programs in the health and education professions and create innovative professional programs, like its Teacher Residency Program.[175]

Some academic highlights during Cline's administration thus far include the creation of Centers of Excellence within the School of Business and the School of Education's receipt of the largest "Race to the Top" grant in New York State ($2.4 million) for the cultivation of effective secondary school mathematics teachers. The School of Education also began efforts to establish a doctoral program and entered into a partnership with the Austrian-American Educational Cooperation Association to offer courses in Europe. Additionally, the College's School of Health and Natural Sciences continued to maintain an impressive 95 percent employment rate for graduates in its graduate degree programs. In 2011, Mercy also opened its Center for Global Engagement to foster international education and invigorate the College's curricula with a global focus by expanding existing global educational programs (like its Model UN program and UN Ambassador's Club Lecture Series), encouraging study abroad programs, increasing international student engagement and sponsoring a new international relations degree program.[176] In addition, Mercy continued to retain and develop new affiliations with other academic institutions and specialized agencies to offer innovative programs.

With Mercy's new support programs, affordability and established academic reputation, Cline's tenure as president quickly became characterized by unprecedented increases in enrollment that created "a new vibrancy" on Mercy's campuses. A rising number of students wishing

Banners depicting Mercy College's current logo ornament the Dobbs Ferry Campus. *Photograph by E. Martone.*

to dorm on campus resulted in the College renting space at local hotels and making plans to increase student housing.[177] In several press interviews, Deirdre Whitman, vice-president of enrollment management, noted several distinctions that attract people to Mercy: "Our very broad course offering. With more than 90 academic programs, the sky is the limit on academic options...Our Personalized Achievement Contract is [also] a drawing card of incredible power, in which each qualified student is paired with a personal mentor...[Further, by] design we offer the lowest private college tuition in metropolitan New York. Mercy College students will not be buried in debt when they graduate." Cline echoed these sentiments in interviews and emphasized Mercy's commitment to not only making a quality education affordable to highly motivated students but also "providing the right suite of services and support to help students complete their degrees and transition successfully into their chosen careers."[178]

The College's commitment to putting students first has resulted in outstanding recognition from a number of prestigious sources. Mercy's academic reputation continued to soar as it attracted increased and repeated national attention as a "college of distinction" in the areas of engaged students, great teaching, vibrant communities and successful outcomes. The College's prestigious Honors Program was named a "Smart Choice" by Peterson's *Honors Programs and Colleges Guide*. Mercy was also repeatedly recognized as a "top military friendly school" by *G.I. Jobs* magazine. *Hispanic Outlook* magazine's list of top one hundred colleges for Hispanics also included Mercy. Further, Mercy's online programs continued to match flexibility with academic quality—in 2005, Mercy received the Alfred Sloan Award for excellence in online teaching and learning.[179]

Mercy's financial health also rose rapidly. Indeed, Mercy has enjoyed its greatest financial position in its entire history under Cline's leadership. The College accumulated substantial increases in total revenues from operating activities, while operating expenses remained steady. Mercy continued to draw substantial local and federal government grants and donations from private foundations. In 2012, Mercy received its first ever "A" credit rating by Standard & Poor's rating services.[180] The College's trustees and former trustees also continued to make generous financial contributions to Mercy. For example, in 2010, Alberto Vitale donated substantial funds for the creation of the Vitale Life Skills Lab, located within the Dunn Center for Student Success and Engagement in Main Hall.[181] Sometimes, trustees attempted to raise financial contributions under creative circumstances. In 2012, for example, trustee Julio Garcia ('87) and Dr. William Martinov Jr., executive director of institutional advancement, formed "Team Mercy" to run in the ING New York City Marathon with the intention of raising funds to endow a new scholarship. Their plans, however, were postponed due to Superstorm Sandy.

The College also began several facility improvements and took action on deferred maintenance needs, primarily on the main campus. Consequently, Main Hall and Mercy Hall were resurfaced in red brick and given new energy-efficient windows. In addition, the newly formed office of student services in Mercy Hall was reconfigured and renovated to provide students more efficient, one-stop service, while Main Hall's interiors were renovated and updated to reinvigorate the building for the twenty-first century. In addition to constant technology upgrades, the Hudson View Café was also refurbished with a new, modern lounge area. One of the most spectacular renovations to the main campus has been the development of the College's dynamic Library Learning Commons, which opened in 2009. The state-of-the art facility unites the library, Mercy Online and the new Faculty Center for Teaching and Learning in an inviting and interactive space to promote intellectual collaboration.[182] In 2012, the College made still further

The Library Learning Commons at the Dobbs Ferry Campus. *Courtesy of the* Impact.

Opposite, bottom: Mercy College's White Plains Branch Campus, which opened during the 1970s, closed in 2012. *Mercy College, Public Relations.*

improvements, including the installation of a state-of-the-art athletic turf field overlooking the Hudson, the renovation of the bookstore and new labs on several campuses.

In 2011, the College formally added a new building to the main campus. The Sisters of Mercy closed OLVA and entered into a long-term rental arrangement with the College, enabling it to use the facility as part of its campus. The College later announced plans to purchase the facility in 2013. With the addition of Victory Hall, six of the eight Mount Mercy buildings became united under the auspices of Mercy College. At about the same time, Mercy unveiled, but eventually withdrew, plans to construct several new academic buildings in front of Verrazzano Hall and an addition for meetings and conferences, as well as to renovate more of Mercy Hall for student housing. Meanwhile, in 2012, BronxNet announced plans to build a TV studio at Mercy's Bronx Campus to provide technological access and media production training. That same year, Mercy decided to close its White Plains Campus and transition the classes, services and programs offered at the White Plains Campus to the main campus.[183]

Mercy College is no stranger to television and film crews. During the fall 2011 semester, Victory Hall was transformed for scenes of the film *The English Teacher*, starring Nathan Lane. Scenes for the television series *Law & Order* were also filmed at Verrazzano Hall for the 2008 episode "Executioner." Other films shot on or around campus include *Falling in Love* (1984), *The Age of Innocence* (1993) and *Unfaithful* (2002). *Photograph by E. Martone.*

Amid the College's growth, Cline's administration witnessed some changes in upper administration and board leadership. In 2009, for example, Gary W. Brown became the new chair of the board of trustees.[184] In 2011, the College created the post of vice-provost and brought in Dr. Graham Glynn from Stony Brook University. The following year, Dr. Concetta Stewart replaced Dr. Michael Sperling as provost and VP for academic affairs.

TABLE 3. CHAIRS OF THE BOARD OF TRUSTEES (1970–PRESENT)

William Stoutenburgh	1969–1970
Robert McCooey	1970–1978
Frederick Kleisner	1978–1980
Walter Anderson	1980–1988
William A. Rose Jr.	1988–1991
Wanda Borges	1991–1995
Francis Ronnenberg	1995–1999
Edward B. Dunn	1999–2006
Richard E. French Jr.	2006–2009
Gary W. Brown	2009–

Cline's tenure as president has also been notable for its increase in alumni events and activities. During the fall 2008 semester, the College commemorated the beginning of Founders' Day for Mercy alumni, faculty, staff and friends. Mary Lyon, widow of Frank Lyon, received Mercy's inaugural Founders' Day Medal, which recognizes individuals who have contributed to the College's growth and development. The late Frank Lyon created the Daddy Short Legs Scholarship to benefit Mercy students. The Grow Garden, named for longtime faculty member and administrator Dr.

Ann Grow, was also announced at that time.[185] The Annual Golf Classic, held at the Ardsley Country Club, has also become a popular event for Mercy alumni, faculty, staff and friends.[186]

Finally, Cline, drawing on Mercy's "long legacy of leadership and innovation that extends beyond its classrooms," has encouraged a return to Mercy's traditional emphasis on service to the community. As Sister Agnes recalled in her early history of Mercy, the College's first president, Sister Mary Gratia Maher, wanted to "make Mercy College an instrument for special services…Its primary purpose as a quality teaching experiment remained, but it was assumed there was also an obligation to undertake projects that could be socially useful to the community."

Revitalizing a secular continuation of these values, Cline quickly sought ways to nurture positive working relationships with the communities in which Mercy campuses reside and inaugurated Mercy's annual Bronx Leadership Dinner. Mercy has launched countless initiatives and programs to serve its host communities, including the development of the School of Education's Parent Center, which held its grand opening at the Bronx Campus in September 2012, and the creation of "Rivertown Parents," a partnership between local parents and Mercy to offer parent education and family support. In cooperation with Bronx Borough president Ruben Diaz Jr. and Bronx-based Truman High School, Mercy has also launched the Bronx Achievement Pact to help raise high school graduation rates, to better prepare students for college and to maximize the number of students enrolling in higher education. As Cline remarked to the press, "A quality education is the critical factor in achieving economic success, personal satisfaction and social stability…The Bronx Achievement Pact will improve educational outcomes for Bronx students and secure a better and more prosperous future for generations of Bronx residents. We are excited to undertake this revolutionary initiative with our committed partners, and we look forward to further collaboration with additional partners as we move ahead."

Meanwhile, the College continued to provide programs for local high school students, such as its Model UN program, a Summer Entrepreneurship Program, an Athletic Camp and a Future Business Leaders Academy. The College has also hosted community events, sports teams, a Destination Imagination program, free lectures, international film screenings, Relays for Life and Big Brother/Big Sister activities. Cline also launched the Mercy College Gives Back campaign, "a college-wide initiative aimed at celebrating and promoting community service at Mercy," and announced

A view of the Hudson from the Dobbs Ferry Campus parking lot. *Courtesy of the* Impact.

the first annual Mercy Day of Service in 2012.[187] Consequently, a trace of the Sisters' influence on the institution can be seen in such service initiatives, as well as in the College's commitment to making education accessible to motivated students.

Mercy continues to enjoy an unprecedented reputation for success. According to former president Dr. Donald Grunewald, Mercy's current success owes much to Cline's exceptional leadership. "I give her a lot of credit," he remarked in an interview. "In my opinion, she ranks among the top presidents in the College's history." Mercy thrives because of the commitment and dedication of the people, like Cline and the numerous members of the faculty, staff and student body, involved in the College's growth and development. When Dr. Ann Grow, who has taught at Mercy for all but thirteen years of its existence, was asked why she stayed at Mercy for so long, her answer was simple: "I'm proud to be part of an unbelievable institution from its earliest days, one that provided opportunity to anyone who really wanted it. You can't get bored with that kind of opportunity, and I've made great friends along the way."[188] Indeed, Mercy is an exceptional college that has left its mark not only on the history of higher education in New York State but also in the hearts of all those who have helped shape and continue to shape its destiny.

Chapter 4
THE SOCIAL SCENE

While academics are an integral part of a student's progression, college is also time to foster and nurture social growth. A college without clubs and activities, and students not behaving passionately in them, is not a true college. It is within these activities that students form bonds that create lifelong friendships and relationships. These special moments are just as important to a student's development as lectures or class assignments.

Mercy's early club activities featured an array of liberal arts performances. Absent, though, were domestic clubs that taught cooking and sewing. As instituted by the College's Social Committee, early clubs emphasized creativity and included glee clubs, poetry readings and coed dances with neighboring men's colleges. The chorus often traveled to West Point, and the ladies of Mercy were not too shy to dress up and perform comedy routine sketches. The Fashion Show and Halloween Party were anticipated events. The Mercy College Players musical club poured its heart out to the students, who began to host the unofficial "Beach Party" on the property behind old Christie Hall near the Hudson.[189] "Mercy Beach" was often a social getaway for students and faculty alike, as the College hosted campfires and cookouts. The location was also renowned for its tranquil setting, as a group of Sisters gathered there on June 7, 1968, to hold a late-night wake for Robert F. Kennedy, who had been killed the day earlier.[190]

Boarders Club Folk In, Class Jeopardy, the Ravineers' Square Dance, Monte Carlo Night and the "Love In" were a few of the many events held during the late 1960s.[191] Traditions were beginning to take shape,

Mercy College's Dobbs Ferry Campus once included property leading to the Hudson. This property was often the site of student leisure activities, barbecues and splash parties. *Mercy College Library Archives.*

During the 1980s, the Mercy College Games allowed students from the College's different campuses to compete in friendly athletic rivalries to promote school spirit. Pictured here are members of the Dobbs Ferry team, whose members sported "Nobody Dobbs it better" T-shirts for the occasion. *Mercy College Library Archives.*

Previous, bottom: Many rituals developed at Mercy College to accompany the upcoming commencement exercises. In 1965, during Class Night, the College held its first Candle and Ivy Celebration. During this ritual, pictured here, seniors passed a candle, representing the light of wisdom, to their sister class, together with ivy, a symbol of friendship. By the end of the 1960s, traditional commencement activities included Class Night ceremonies, a senior formal, a Baccalaureate Day Mass and luncheon, dinner and theater party, a splash party and the actual commencement exercises. *Mercy College Library Archives.*

including the annual Sports Day, where faculty and students faced off in events around campus, like basketball games, softball and sprint races. This event changed over the years as campuses began competing against one another in the annual Mercy Sports Day.[192] Mercy also borrowed some rituals from West Point Military Academy. Before Mercy became coed, Mercy and West Point occasionally ran social mixers together. Borrowed were the concepts of Ring Day and 101 Nights. At West Point, seniors have a party one hundred days before graduation. Until 1974, Mercy's women hosted 101 Nights, in which the junior class entertained the senior class with comedy sketches and a talent show.[193] The Halloween Party, in the past referred to as Masquerade Night or the Masquerade Ball, is still for the most part a Mercy annual tradition.

"The Pub," as it was known to Mercy students, was located where the current Occupational and Physical Therapy offices are situated. The Pub, independently owned, was open from 11:00 a.m. to 10:00 p.m., Monday through Friday. According to reports in the *Reporter's Impact*, many students celebrated their birthdays in the Pub. In 1982, the drinking age was raised from eighteen to nineteen. On December 1, 1985, the drinking age was elevated to age twenty-one. Shortly thereafter, the bar was closed, and Student Services initiated a policy that many colleges nationwide were also enforcing.[194] Mercy was deemed a dry campus, a policy that still stands today.

THE YEARBOOK

A yearbook, featuring headshots of participating seniors and photos of the academic school year, was published from 1965 up until 1994.

In its early days, the yearbook was known simply as *The Annual*. Every issue was hardbound and typically dedicated to a faculty member or administrator who had touched the students' lives. Photos of students and Sisters laughing, dancing and studying swarmed the pages. Every page was full of life and hope, a tradition that lasted until the publication ceased.

As times changed, so did *The Annual*. Song lyrics, movie quotes and news headlines became more prevalent, making the yearbooks truly capsules of their era. Within a few years, *The Annual* name was dropped, and most yearbooks became individually named. In the late 1980s, the yearbook itself would be named the *Blue Max* in reference to the life-size artwork still displayed on campus and the blue and white colors of Mercy.

Mercy College's seal, designed by William Ryan, a master of ecclesiastical and secular heraldry, reflects the College's history and location. It is composed of a shield, motto and external ornaments. The gold cross in a red field above red and gold bars is the emblem of the Sisters of Mercy. The red saltire (X) over a silver field is the cross of St. Patrick, patron of Ireland, where the order of the Sisters of Mercy was founded. The two open books represent the College's goals, namely to open or broaden minds with the transformative power of education. The crest of the four-sailed windmill represents the Hudson Valley by recalling its early Dutch history. The Latin motto can be translated as "to be consumed in service." *Mercy College Library Archives.*

As the staff of *Yearbook '76* put it, Mercy's yearbook "is created by a group of interested students who wish to develop a profile of life at Mercy. The yearbook staff strives to give recognition to the seniors who have successfully achieved their degrees and to the faculty who aided in this achievement. Mainly, it strives in bringing forth the involvement and spirit of all students in attendance at Mercy."[195]

Mercy's inaugural *Annual* was printed for the 1965 graduating class. The initial editor in chief was Roseann Vierno, and the staff consisted of more than thirty-three student volunteers. The dedication read, "To the college which has bequeathed us the most precious gift of Christian wisdom, and to those persons whose forethought and untiring efforts have made possible that College, the class of 1965 dedicate its first Annual."[196]

In 1968, song lyrics from Bob Dylan appeared as *The Annual* embraced the social upheavals that were occurring inside and outside Mercy's walls. In 1969, *The Annual* received an individual title for the first time: *Hedera*. A hedera is an ivy plant that is fragile, but like a student, it can reach great heights if supported. The 1970 annual, named *Blueprints*, continued that tradition. Within these pages, students showed their creative and lighthearted nature.[197]

In 1971, the annual began to be referred to as a yearbook. Entitled *Mankind*, it was the first time that national issues, notably woman's lib protests and Kent State, were featured in a Mercy yearbook. Titles in the

Perhaps surprisingly, helicopters are not an unusual sight on a Mercy campus. For example, on January 17, 1981, a military helicopter, on its way to Washington, D.C., from Cape Cod, made an emergency landing at the Dobbs Ferry Campus parking lot. John Mulheren, a relative of Dr. Frances Mahoney, also frequently arrived via helicopter, usually for convent events. *Mercy College Library Archives.*

coming years included *Changes* and *Reflections* in 1972 and 1973, respectively. Song lyrics, like from Peter, Paul and Mary's "Leaving on a Jet Plane" and the Youngbloods' "Get Together," addressed the political climate. A picture of a student's bumper sticker read:

Make Wine, Not War
—Hudson Valley Wine.

The 1975 yearbook, titled *Metamorphisis*, was the first to feature color. Later titles were *Crossroads*, *Stars*, *Currents*, *Bursting Out* and *The Travelers*.

In 1984, the *On Broadway* edition was the first yearbook to publish original stories, some of which were reprinted from the *Reporter's Impact*. Some notable articles were Richard Read's reluctant rant about Mercy fashions and Donna Bisetto's endorsement of cable television, which was available in 1984 for twenty dollars per month.[198]

Future titles included *Putting the Pieces Together*, *In Transition* and *On the Horizon*. In 1988, the annual took the title *The Blue Max*, and the volume was named "On the Move: The Golden Year," in reference to Mercy's Golden Commencement. In 1989, the volume was entitled "The Final Countdown." The last yearbook referred to as *The Blue Max* was the 1991 edition. The yearbook lasted only three more years and was considerably smaller, void of color and held little more than headshots of seniors.

Clubs

The Accounting Society, advised by Professor Lucretia Mann, was founded in 2005 to help students gain valuable insight from guest lecturers, alumni, faculty and fellow students on how to prepare for a career in the accounting profession. The club's business etiquette training event and the Volunteer Income Tax Assistance program have become popular Mercy experiences. The club also sponsors presentations that have exposed students to career paths in the field of accounting. These presentations led to fifteen accounting students being placed in the Big 4 first from 2009 to 2012.[199]

The Black Student Union (BSU), created in 1998 and reintroduced to the campus in the spring of 2009, is advised by Terrance V. Jackson. The BSU's mission is to encourage cultural unity and awareness and enhance the

Through active participation in various student clubs and activities, Mercy students have acquired a renowned reputation for their contributions to the community. In this yearbook photograph, a group of Mercy College students marches in a local Columbus Day parade during the 1970s. *Mercy College Library Archives.*

education benefits for all members of Mercy's student body and community. The BSU annually sponsors the Mercy's Got Talent student showcase, the open-mic night Mercy Speaks, an AIDS awareness colloquium and a Kwanzaa celebration. The BSU participates in the African American Parade, Step Out: Walk to Stop Diabetes and Making Strides Against Breast Cancer, as well as food and clothing drives.[200]

The Child Abuse Prevention Center Collegiate Club (CAPCCC), founded in March 2003 in collaboration with the National Exchange Club, is advised by Dr. Dorothy Balancio, Lindsay Astor and Chelsea Kuo. The club's purpose is to provide opportunities and development for student volunteers by promoting active participation in service to the prevention of child abuse. The club holds annual Thanksgiving, Christmas and Mother's Day events for the community. After completing the Child Abuse Prevention Center training, many student volunteers become "parent aids" in the community. The club has received substantial recognition from the CAPC.[201]

GLOW UP, or the "Gay, Lesbian Or Whatever U Prefer" club, is an incarnation of the Gay Straight Alliance, which went inactive in 2011 after many years of service. The group was revived in 2012 by adviser Jose Barzola

Mercy College has always been a student-centered institution. In this 1980s photograph, Mercy faculty and students engage in lively conversation. *Mercy College Library Archives.*

and current student adviser Kimberly Lindermann. The club is open to anyone who wishes to attend and is designed to assist, celebrate, support and create a safe environment for the Mercy campus. The club aims to join with anyone who is gay, lesbian, bisexual, transgender, straight or uncertain of how to classify him or herself. The club has also been active in local breast cancer and diabetes walks.[202]

The HELP campus ministry, founded in 2011, is advised by Joe Cooke. The club aims to have the campus get in touch with its "spiritual side" and sponsors Bible study sessions, worship ceremonies and community service projects.[203]

The *Impact*, the college newspaper, was established in the 1960s and is advised by Professor Michael Perrota. The periodical prints a variety of news stories and profiles focusing on the topics of campus life, the college experience and New York events. The paper's online counterpart, theimpactnews.com, was launched in 2011 and features online-only content, notably the columns of the *Impact* staff writers. In recent years, the *Impact* has won several individual and staff awards. In 2007, the New York Press Association awarded Katherine Ryan's article on "The War on Terror" second in the category of News Reporting. In 2009, the American Scholastic Press Association (ASPA) awarded Ryan a first-place award for editorial writing. The following year, Jennifer Lagrippo won first-place honors in the *USA Today* College News Reporting Contest for her story about the study drug Adderall. In 2011, the ASPA awarded Jessi Rucker first-place honors in the "Feature Writing" category for her story about her voyage to Vietnam.[204]

The *Impact* began as a club and printed a broadsheet-style newspaper throughout the semesters. Its original title was *Town and Gown*. The office was located in a conference room on the third floor of Main Hall. Typically, appointments as the editor in chief were given to a senior, who would then step down in April to a junior classmate selected to assume the position the following academic year. The editor, Nona Peterson, along with her staff, decided to change the publication's title to the *M.C. Image*. The first issue of the *M.C. Image* was printed on May 1, 1970. The title would only stick for two issues, ending with the May 15, 1970 edition.[205]

Doug Otis, possibly Mercy's first admitted male student when it became coed, recommended to Peterson while serving as a reporter on the *M.C. Image* that the paper change its name to the *Impact*. In an interview, he stated that he attended a September 24, 1970 meeting in Main Hall over student concern about a lack of campus parking. He claimed that tensions escalated, and he felt that the newspaper should reflect the impact of events on campus. He drew up an initial logo, and the first issue of the *Impact* was printed later that week.[206]

In 1977, Dr. Paul Thaler became the newspaper's adviser, and the *Impact* was rebranded as the *Reporter's Impact*. That year, the paper became officially associated with the journalism program under the English department. The paper did not publish in 2002. In 2003, it was renamed the *Impact* and ran as a magazine once a semester. In 2004, it returned as a multi-issue newspaper in tabloid size.[207]

Other Mercy student publications include the *Mavericks' Education Journal: An Innovative Guide to Teaching*, a journal produced by graduate students in the School of Education. The journal's first issue, with faculty adviser Dr. Eric Martone, was published in 2012.

Professor Alan Hartman revived the Italian Club in 2007 to disseminate an increased awareness of the Italian and Italian American cultures on campus. The club hosts an annual "Italian Night," where guest speakers and the community share discussion about Italian culture.[208]

The Lions Club, chartered on June 24, 2009, is advised by Professor Susan Gunser and sponsored by the Yonkers Lions Cub. Its mission statement, as

Members of the Mercy College community, especially its students, have traditionally maintained an extensive commitment to community service. One such organization is the Mercy College chapter of the Lions Club, which allows members to provide humanitarian service to the local, national and global communities. This photograph was taken at the Mercy College Lions Club's first annual Pancake Breakfast. *Dr. Paul Gunser, vice-president of the Yonkers Lions Club.*

is the mission statement of the international organization that was founded in 1917, is "We Serve." The Lions Club initially aimed to serve the visually impaired, but it also serves others in need locally, nationally and globally. The Mercy chapter runs an annual eyeglasses recycling fund and participates in a military gifting program to combat troops in Afghanistan. The club hosts monthly bake sales in which proceeds are donated to the American Cancer Society, Autism Speaks and the Wounded Warrior Project. Mercy's Lions Club has been recognized by Lions Club Multiple District 20R2 as a successful campus club.[209]

Adam Parmenter advises the Maverick Society, founded as part of the 2010–11 Senior Class Gift Campaign. The club is a collection of students fundraising toward the Annual Fund, which supports Mercy students' long-term success. The society takes a role in campus-wide initiatives, like the Senior Class gift, and has sponsored recycling programs, a change drive, dances, car washes and bake sales to support scholarships. In its first year, the society recycled nearly twenty thousand bottles and cans on campus.[210]

Professor Rick Shiels created the College's Model United Nations Team in 1986. The team earns college credit by competing in the annual national Model UN conference held in Manhattan. Mercy has represented more than twenty-five countries, including nations from Africa, Latin American and Europe.[211]

The No Mercy Step Team, founded in 2007, is advised by Joe Cooke and provides entertainment, activities and expression for students, faculty and the College community. The team competes in talent shows, step competitions and community service projects. It received the BSU's Certificate of Appreciation in 2012.[212]

Rotaract, created in 2010, is a local branch of the Rotary International Club and is advised by Jasmine Dumas. It seeks to provide opportunities for young men between the ages of eighteen and thirty to enhance their skills and knowledge in personal development and address the physical and social needs of the community. The club also aims to promote better relations between all people worldwide through a framework of friendship and service. It participates in the Relay for Life Walkathon, Making Strides Against Breast Cancer and the Step Out: Walk to Stop Diabetes. The club sponsors a Midnight Run food drive, blood drives and annual on-site HIV testing. The club participates in the Children's Village Mentoring Program and arts and crafts days at Maria Fareri Children's Hospital and volunteers at the Salvation Army Food Pantry and Soup Kitchen. The club earned a 2010–11 Presidential Citation from Rotary International.[213]

The Social Work Club, created in 2011, is advised by Dr. Nicholas Forge to establish a social work presence on campus through advocacy, education and volunteerism. The club also promotes a positive self-image for the profession and encourages its members to assume responsibility in identifying the need for social change and actively participate in facilitating such a change. The club has participated in AIDS and breast cancer walks, raised funds for Autism Speaks and supported the New Yorkers for Children literacy and college readiness workshop for foster care children. It has also partnered with the Bread and Life Agency in Brooklyn to provide toiletries and baby supplies.[214]

The Speech-Language-Hearing Club, founded in the 1960s, is advised by Dr. Gloria Schlisselberg. It is a chapter of the National Student Speech-Language-Hearing Association (NSSLHA). The club promotes interest among students in the study of normal and disordered communication through social, fundraising and educational events. The club hosts monthly bingo evenings at the St. Cabrini Skilled Nursing Facility and the Westchester

In September 1967, Mercy College developed a Child Center for children with special needs. However, the Child Center quickly placed a large financial strain on the College, which was advised to "eliminate peripheral programs" to better secure approval from Middle States. Despite some assistance from the local community and public fundraising events, a plan to phase the center out was put in place in 1969. The Child Center served as the inspiration for the development of Mercy College's Speech and Hearing Center, which has served the community for more than twenty-five years with comprehensive diagnostic evaluations and therapy for children and adults. *Mercy College Library Archives.*

Chapter of the HLAA's Walk 4 Hearing. It also sponsors the Embassy Community Center Discussion Group. The club has earned bronze chapter status from the national HSSLHA office.[215]

Students Against Destructive Decisions (SADD), created in 2012, is advised by Nick Canzano. The club provides students with prevention tools to deal with issues like underage drinking, drug use and risky or impaired driving, among other destructive decisions.[216]

The Student Government Association (SGA) has undergone many transformations throughout Mercy's history. Revived in 2011, it is advised by Jose Barzola. In 2012, the new SGA's elections resulted in the appointments of an executive board that included Althea Brown, president; Freedom Weeks, vice-president; Dawn Henderson, secretary; and Glenroy Wason, treasurer. The SGA, the voice of the student body, plans social events and represents students' views within the College. Officials are student elected and manage committees and councils to represent students' general welfare.

The SGA meets to discuss current campus issues and concerns. SGA created the Student Leadership Council, in which one member of every club meets together monthly to increase communication between clubs. Also created was the Student Engagement Forum, a venue in which students can voice their opinions twice a semester regarding issues they are facing.[217]

Today's Believers Tomorrow's Leaders (TBTL), also advised by Jose Barzola, was founded in 2012 and works with upper- and lower-class students to advise them on future career choices and inspirations. TBTL offers mentors to students and leadership training, sponsors food and clothing drives and hosts career professionals to speak to interested students about their chosen fields.[218]

The Veterans Club, founded in 2000, is advised by Joe Cooke. The club reaches out to veteran students to have them participate in special projects helping current and returning troops.[219]

Additional clubs include the Corporate and Homeland Security Club, Caribbean Student Association, Intensified Image Dance Team, Cheerleading Club, Science Club, Creative Minds Poetry Club, Honors Club, Veterinary Technology Club, Computer Club and the National Society of Collegiate Scholars of Mercy College.

Defunct clubs include the Glee Club, which performed on campus and at other colleges, such as Iona and Columbia (the club also performed annually at the Waldorf as part of the Christmas program of the Metropolitan Opera Guild); the Mercy College Players, which performed musicals and plays such as *The Sound of Music*, *All the Way Home*, *You Know I Can't Hear You When the Water Is Running* and *The Crucible*; the History Club, which produced the first seven members of Mercy's chapter (Phi Zeta) of Phi Alpha Theta, the international honor society for history, in 1974; the Outdoors Club, introduced in the 1970s as an attempt to introduce students to canoeing, horseback riding and camping; the Middle Eastern Society, which was dedicated to finding a mutual understanding between Middle Eastern and American cultures; the Modern Foreign Languages Club, which sought to raise awareness about cultures found in Romance-language countries and held an Italian Fiesta; and the Third World Union, created in the early 1970s, initially to "provide an awareness to the students of the black cause in today's world"—in 1978, its mission shifted, resulting in the creation of the BSU, and a decade later, the African Heritage Club was formed.

Other defunct clubs include the Anime Club, Mercy College Models, French Club, Performing Faces Drama Club, Republican Club, Ski Club, Circle K, Meerskellar Club, Fraternity of Music Students, Photography

Mercy College has long been home to a diverse student body. Mirroring trends in broader U.S. immigration, the College began to acquire larger numbers of Asian and Asian American students. As part of its tradition of developing innovative programs to meet local needs, the College began to offer bilingual programs for Korean students. In this 1990s photograph, Korean students enjoy a picnic on campus. *Mercy College Library Archives.*

Club, Film Club, Football Club, Criminal Justice Club, Students for Social Consciousness, Programming Board Club, Radio Club, Speech Club, Mathematics Club, Gaelic Club, Latin Club, Spoken Wheel, Martial Arts Club, International Student Association, Vet Tech Club, New Social Enterprise Club, Irish Society, Tri-Beta/MACE (Mercy Against Corruption of the Environment) and the Public Safety Club.

Many honor societies have flourished at Mercy. Phi Beta Kappa, the country's oldest honor society, was charted in 1979 and was advised by Dr. Nancy Benson. Sigma Phi Sigma and Delta Mu Delta, also known as the Business Administration National Society, began inducting members in 1975. Sr. Agnes O'Grady acted as the initial advisor to the club. Chapters of Pi Gamma Mu, the Social Science Honor Society, and Kappa Delta Pi, the education honor society, were founded in 1977. A chapter of Psi Chi, the psychology honor society, was founded in 1978, and Lambda Iota Tau, the honor society for literature, was founded in 1980 under adviser Dr. Nancy Benson. Phi Sigma Iota, also known as the Modern Foreign Language

Society, was created in 1974. Fourteen members were inducted under Dr. Thomas Vesce, chair of the Department of Foreign Languages.[220]

All programs in the School of Health and Natural Sciences participate in the Alpha Eta National Honor Society. Other honor societies at Mercy are Beta Beta Beta, for biology; Pi Alpha, for physician assistants; Sigma Theta Tau, for nursing; and Pi Mu Epsilon, for math.

Mercy students have produced two radio stations. The initial station, WMCY, was initiated on January 30, 1984, and run by the Radio Club and its adviser, Gary Axelbank. It took three years of student fundraising led by Tom Brandt, who had dreams of hosting a radio show.[221] The show ran a top forty format and sought paid advertising under the leadership of students like Brian Price, Chip Beaman and Laura Dermer. Frank DeNunzio emerged as a prominent disc jockey during the late 1980s. The relationship between students and faculty was often uneasy, and the station eventually ceased broadcasting in the mid-1990s. In 2001, Mercy entered into a five-year partnership with WDFH (90.3) and its license owner and executive director, Professor Marc Sophos. A studio was designed in Main Hall for $250,000, and the station started broadcasting in the fall of 2003.[222] The station earned national recognition for its political coverage and aired a three-hour September 11 anniversary program with interviews of eyewitnesses. Due to its $40,000 a year upkeep and enrollment that did not meet expectations, Mercy did not extend the station's contract, and the agreement ceased on June 30, 2006.[223]

EVENTS

Christie Day was initiated on May 6, 1984, in honor of Sister Mary Joannes Christie, the founder of the English department. Dr. Fay Greenwald, chair of the Department of Literature, Language and Communications, instituted the honors of the Joannes Christie Award, a silver bowl given annually to an outstanding student of English literature, as well as the Annual Shakespeare Lecture, given in honor of Sister Joannes. At the inaugural event, Sister Joanes presented a lecture titled, "Shakespeare: Not for an Age but for All Time." Traditionally, students, faculty and professionals perform readings from Shakespearean plays in her honor. The event is presently coordinated by Dr. Frances Biscoglio.

Dr. Maria Enrico established the International Film Festival in 1999. It is presented by the School of Liberal Arts in association with the Center for

Global Engagement, PACT, the Center for Student Success and Engagement, the Honors Program and the offices of the provost and president. The event cultivates knowledge of foreign cultures to the students, faculty and Mercy community. Five films are shown in April annually and hosted by guest speakers. The event, open to the public, is currently coordinated by Dr. Ellen Kreger.

Sister Mary Joannes Christie during the early 1960s. *Mercy College Library Archives.*

The Quill Awards, established in 1983 by Paul Thaler, are affiliated with the media studies program. It is currently run by Louis Grasso. Students are honored for exceptional course work. Annually, plaques are given to the winners of the Alumni Quill Award and the Quill Award for Professional Achievement. Notable guest speakers and winners of the Professional Achievement Award have been ABC's Sandra Bookman, CNN's Jeff Greenfield, *Sports Illustrated*'s Jeff Pearlman, NBC's Len Berman and WFAN's Chris Russo.[224]

Speechfest is an annual public speaking competition launched in 1988 under Paul Trent. Five finalists compete, delivering four- to six-minute speeches of any design—persuasive, informative or argumentative. Students are encouraged to be extemporaneous and use visual aids. Cash prizes are awarded for the top three speechmakers. The competition is judged by a panel consisting of the head of the English department, a speech professor and an outside guest. Notable speeches have been presented on topics like race relations, gay and women's rights, abortion, the criminal justice system and the environment. Speechfest's precursor, The Soap Box, a competition that resembled a debate format, debuted three years previously.

Chapter 5

ATHLETICS

In 1963, Mercy played its first official varsity game—women's basketball. It was the genesis to a tradition of majestic athletes wearing white and blue representing their college proudly and impressively. Mercy was victorious that day, setting a high standard of success and gamesmanship that is followed by every athlete who has called himself or herself a Flyer or Maverick.

In 1970, the men's basketball team tipped off, and male athletics at Mercy ushered in a new era of College expansion and growth. Mercy currently has ten NCAA Division II sports teams: men's and women's basketball, men's and women's lacrosse, baseball, softball, field hockey, women's volleyball and men's and women's soccer.

The oldest sports organization at Mercy is the cheerleading program, which began early in the 1960s, as female students had participated in cheering at their high schools. In 1965, with no male teams to support, the cheerleading club became the official cheerleaders for Iona College and, as former athletic director Neil Judge remembers it, "cheer[ed] on their boyfriends."[225]

Judge joined Mercy as a physical education instructor in 1969. By 1971, he had become the College's first athletic director, a position he would hold for thirty-four years. His hard work allowed Mercy to be accepted to the Eastern Collegiate Athletic Conference in 1973. Two years later, the National Collegiate Athletic Assocation (NCAA) initiated Mercy, a feat that many credit to Judge and his staff.[226]

On October 3, 2005, Dr. Kevin T. McGinniss became the second athletic director in Mercy history after serving as Quinnipiac's director of athletic development. In 2008, Patricia Kennedy, former head women's basketball coach and field hockey coach at C.W. Post and former women's athletic director as LIU, assumed the position as athletic director.

Mercy joined the charter members of the New York Collegiate Athletic Conference (NYCAC) in 1989 with Adelphi University, Concordia College, C.W. Post College, Dowling College, Molloy College, New York Institute of technology (NYIT), Pace University, Queens College and Southhampton College of LIU. The conference has since changed its name to the East Coast Conference (ECC). Adelphi, Concordia, Pace and Southhampton College have since left the conference. The conference currently has ten teams, with the University of Bridgeport, St. Thomas Aquinas College, the University of the District of Columbia and Roberts Wesleyan College as members. In 2013, Daemen College will join the conference.[227]

Without a true field, Mercy initially practiced on the Our Lady of Victory softball field and played most games on the road or at the Dobbs Ferry High School's field. In the mid-1970s, Westchester County made a financial agreement with Mercy to drop landfill on the large hill that ran from Main Hall to the railroad tracks. After a three-year period, the ground was leveled and then built on with sand, dirt and eventually grass—Mercy's home field

In 2012, Mercy College began construction of a new turf field. *Courtesy of the* Impact.

The "Mercy Flyers" had used an eagle as a mascot, but its use had been phased out by the early 2000s. In 2007, the College unveiled the new "Mavericks" nickname and mascot. *Mercy College, Public Relations.*

was born.[228] In the summer of 2012, the original ball fields were demolished, and Mavericks Field was unveiled. The $1.5 million artificial grass renovation gave Mercy a true home field advantage. The field was christened on September 22, 2012, during Mercy's Founders' Day Fall Festival, as the Dobbs Ferry High School football team defeated Pawling, 27–0.[229]

Intramural sports have always been an important aspect of Mercy life. Squads of teams consisted in badminton, basketball, table tennis and volleyball. In the 1977–78 academic year, touch football and coed softball teams were created. That same year, the Village of Dobbs Ferry requested that Mercy take over its adult tennis program, which led to the community using the tennis courts, which still exist today. Outdoor handball and basketball leagues were created and became extremely popular on weekends. For a time, American Legion Baseball used the College's baseball diamond when available.[230] Mercy briefly sponsored an equestrian club in the mid-1980s for four seasons.[231] Flag football, softball and basketball are still played often by Mercy students.

On May 15, 2007, then athletic director Kevin McGinniss announced that Mercy would change its mascot from a Flyer to a Maverick. A committee reviewed suggestions from students, athletes and faculty. Five finalists were chosen: the Mavericks, the Mustangs, the River Hawks, the Cougars and the Wildcats.[232] McGinniss was quoted at the unveiling of the new mascot as saying, "A maverick is someone who exhibits great independence in thought and action—a maverick is a leader. The nickname Mavericks truly embodies the spirit of Mercy College and Mercy College athletics. It's a nickname that the entire Mercy community can be proud of and rally around."[233]

WOMEN'S BASKETBALL

The women's basketball team, Mercy's inaugural sport team, was coached by Eileen McMahon and played its first game on December 4, 1963. The team pounced Dominican, 49–10. After losses to Seton and Marymount, the team won its final two games by defeating St. John's, 32–27, and Good Counsel, 37–31. McMahon coached the team for four years, earning an 18-10 record.

The team's best winning percentage was compiled during the 1973–74 season when it posted a 12-1 (.923) record under Neil Judge. The team rattled off 12 straight victories but fell in its final contest. That season began the first of two dominant eras of Mercy College women's basketball.

Judge stepped down after coaching the team for only one season. He was replaced by Cathi Wasilik, who posted a 104-45 (.698) record in six seasons. In the 1974–75 season, the team posted a record of 15-2 (.882) and lost only to one team that season: Iona, twice. The team won its first five games, including a 101–17 thrashing of NYU and a 112–22 victory over Ladycliff. Mercy fell to Iona, 62–46, rebounded by winning ten games in a row and then lost to Iona again in the last game of the season, 72–62.

During the 1975–76 season, the team posted an incredible 24-3 (.889) record, which is still a record for women's basketball wins. The team scored more than one hundred points seven times and is the most formidable team in Mercy history.

The team started the season with twenty-one consecutive victories (also a record) and earned its revenge from the previous season by defeating Iona, 73–63, on February 20. Dubbed on campus as "The Game," it was one of the most anticipated games in program history. The team would lose to Princeton and Salisbury State before defeating Iona once again, 63–61, in the EAIAW Regional Small Basketball Tournament, earning a fourth-place finish.

In the New York state final, the team handed St. John Fisher its only loss of the season, 81–64, and defeated Stony Brook, 58–47. The team suffered a lopsided loss to Long Island in the finals, 69–33, after some team members missed curfew. The team is considered by many to be the most dominant Mercy team in College history.[234]

Four starters averaged double digits. Helen Peros scored 19.6 per game, Mary Brechbiel added 18.3 per game, Kathy Lamberti scored 12.1 per game, Maggie Ferrara scored 11.1 per game and Donna Spafford scored 8.5 points per game while averaging ten rebounds. "They were unguardable. No one had an answer for Helen and Mary," commented Judge. "The team

A 1960s Mercy College girls' basketball team in action. *Mercy College Library Archives.*

moved the ball so well. I've never seen anything like it. Most of their totals are actually deflated, since the team was up by so many points. The starters would only play half a game."[235]

Behind Brechbiel, the 1977–78 team finished 22-10 and made a deep run in the Eastern Association for Intercollegiate Athletics for Women's Northeast regional tournament by defeating Brown, Eastern Connecticut and Yale. The team eventually fell to Fordham.

Wasilik stepped down after the 1980 season. After a one-year stint by Dale Siegal, Carol Schachner-Leib took over the program. She coached for eleven years and earned the most victories ever by a Mercy women's basketball coach by posting a 166-141 (.541) overall record. After a 7-16 start in her inaugural season, she posted a 20-12 record, advanced to the NCAA regional finals and won the Hudson Valley conference crown for the sixth time in College history.[236] It would also be Mercy's final season as a member of the Hudson Valley Women's Athletic Conference.

The team joined the Empire State conference, and the following three years mark the last dominant era of Mercy women's basketball. From the 1983–84 to the 1985–86 season, the team posted records of 22-8, 22-7 and 19-9, losing to Adelphi, Utica and Pace in the NCAA playoffs. The 1982 team defeated Niagara University, 73–65, behind Joyce LeNoir's 18 points in the first round of the State II Division Playoffs but fell to no. 1 seed St. John Fisher, 68–64, in a performance that was considered "gutsy."[237] The 1983–84 team defeated Colgate, 73–70, in the state tournament but lost to Canisius, 77–73, in the final round in Buffalo despite "sparkplug" guard Noreen Annunziata's 18 points.

The following season, the team fell to Pace, 78–67, in the Empire State conference finals. The teams during that era were led by the "Fantastic Four": Stacey Gillespie, Joyce LeNoir, Noreen Annunziata and Ursula Gregg. All four ladies scored more than 1,000 career points in the 1984–85 season. Gillespie was Metropolitan Collegiate Basketball Association player of the year in the 1983–84 season. In the 1986–87 season, the team posted a 6-20 record to suffer its first losing season in five years.

Women's basketball posted a 17-11 record in the 1988–89 season, the last time the team finished with a winning record. The team defeated C.W. Post, 78–62, in the ECC conference semifinals and fell to Molloy, 67–53, in the finals.

In 1990, the team shifted conferences to the New York Collegiate Athletic Conference. The team finished 13-13 in 1998 under Coach Michelle Coyle. It would be nearly twelve years until the team recorded double-digit victories again, as the 2008–9 team went 10-18. The program suffered winless 0-25 seasons in the 2004–5 and 2005–6 seasons.

Stacy Gillespie (1982–86) is Mercy's career leader in points (1,749 points). Behind her are Ursula Gregg (1982–86) with 1,654, Marcy Brechbiel (1974–78) with 1,534, Noreen Annunziata (1982–86) with 1,532 and Christine Baxter (2005–9) with 1,501. Gillespie is also the career leader in rebounds with 1,617. Behind her are Debbie Barnes (1976–80) with 1,391, Corey York (1977–81) with 1,105 and Michelle Coyle (1988–92) with 1,032. Gillespie is also second in all-time field goals with 720, trailing Gregg's 726.

Baxter and Joyce LeNoir (1982–85) are tied for the all-time count in assists with 537. York leads the career list in blocks at 133; Gillespie and Coyle follow at 108. Brechbiel is the all-time leader in steals with 488 and is the first female to earn a Mercy athletic scholarship.

Helen Peros scored the most points in a single season (1977–78) with 548. Niurca Herrera averaged the most points per game with 18.9 in 1995–96 and registered the most successful free throws in one season with 162.[238]

Men's Basketball

The men's basketball team played its first game on November 30, 1970, coached by Athletic Director Neil Judge, against Our Lady of Hope and won in resounding fashion, 87–59. The team finished with an impressive 11-4 record in its inaugural season.

Judge coached the basketball program's first five seasons without a losing season. He accumulated a 71-30 record, the highest winning percentage (.703) for any men's basketball coach. Judge is also the only men's basketball coach to post a career winning record for Mercy.

The program left the ECAC and joined the Knickerbocker Conference. In the 1972–73 season, the team finished with 20-4, which is still the record for most wins in a men's basketball season. The Flyers won eight straight games to start the season, defeating teams like Vassar, John Jay and Manhattanville, until it fell to St. Thomas Aquinas College by a score of 87–48. Mercy responded with another winning streak, 10 games, to cap off the most impressive regular season run in Mercy College men's basketball history. At 18-1, the team split the next four games until it valiantly lost to St. Thomas Aquinas College, 119–103, to end the season. The team avenged its loss by beating St. Thomas Aquinas in the season finale the following season after posting a 13-7 record.

Joseph Flowers became head coach during the 1976–77 season. He recorded four straight winning seasons (17-10, 16-10, 12-10 and 12-10), then posted a .500 season at 12-12 in the 1980–81 season. During the 1977–78 season, Mercy upset the no. 1 ranked team in Division II on February 9, 1978, by a score of 98–90. Mercy defeated NYIT, 102–100, in the Knickerbocker Conference semifinals but lost to Stony Brook in the rematch, 88–82, for the title. The 1980–81 season would be the last year the College's men's basketball program finished .500 or better. The team would come close during the 1992–93 season with a 13-14 record under Head Coach Mike Young (43-121, career) and during the 2004–5 season with a 12-14 record under Head Coach Steve Kelly (77-205, career).

Meanwhile, in 1989, the team moved to the NYCAC, which later renamed itself the ECC. In 1996, Derrick Henry's fifty-two-point performance against Assumption College led to a feature in the March 11 issue of *Sports Illustrated*'s "Faces in the Crowd."[239]

The jerseys of three players are currently retired: Robert Davis, Brian Donohue and Tom Sivulich. Davis (1983–86) is Mercy's all-time leading scorer at 2,118 points. Known as "The Rocket" to his teammates and around

A 1970s Mercy College boys' basketball team photograph including Brian Donohue (12), a 2009 inductee into the Mercy College Athletic Hall of Fame. *Mercy College Library Archives.*

campus, Davis is fourth all time with 373 assists and second in steals with 231. He was a two-time conference selection and Division II All-Metropolitan honoree. Donohue is the second all-time leading scorer in Mercy history with 2,028 points. He was the first player in College history (men's and women's) to score 1,000 points in his career. He also set the Mercy record for most points in a game, 45, against rival St. Thomas Aquinas, a top twenty NAIA team, on February 5, 1977. The team scored 139 points against St. Thomas Aquinas, still a Mercy record. Sivulich's 1,526 points puts him third all time on Mercy's career list. A perimeter shooter, he played without the luxury of a 3-point line. His 667 assists are a College record. Sivulich also owns the single-season record for assists with 18, a mark he set on February 19, 1978, against Dominican. He was a First Team All-Conference and First Team All-ECAC selection.

Frank Bailey is the all-time leader in rebounds with 703. He is trailed by John McMahon at 636 rebounds, Alywnn Waldron (2002–5) at 618 rebounds and Ilee Coleman (1988–92) at 604 rebounds. Coleman is the all-time leader in steals with 261 and games played at 103 and is fourth in points with 1,327. Chris Middleton (1992–95) is the all-time leader in blocked shots with 118. Davis owns three of the four single-season scoring record totals, notably his 1985–86 season in which he scored 617 points. James Harrison set the single-season mark for rebounds with 283 during the 1983–84 season. Derrick Henry, second all time in career assists, set the single-season record in the 1995–96 season with 161. Jermaine Turner (1995–96) and Michael Beaton (2002–3) are tied for most blocks in a single season with 52.[240]

Baseball

Mercy's baseball team began in 1972 under Head Coach Neil Judge. The team posted losing seasons until 1975, when it registered an 11-3 record, its first winning season.

In 1980, Rick Wolff assumed the coaching reins, and the team moved from Division III to Division II. He posted a winning record the following season at 18-10-1, which is also the year Mercy joined the Knickerbocker Conference. As a freshman, pitcher Pat Geoghegan, an eventual Mercy Hall of Famer, pitched a two-hitter against St. Francis, which was Mercy's first victory against a Division I team. During that season, first baseman and team captain Bob Crescenzo hit a game-winning two-run homerun against Pace to win, 5–3. Pace was Division I and a powerhouse in the conference. Judge later referred to it as Mercy's "biggest win ever."[241] Wolff posted four more years of greater than .500 baseball, with records of 18-10, 18-9, 21-12 and 17-10. In 1981, Geoghegan defeated the no. 2 ranked team in the nation, New Haven, 10–5.

In the 1984–85 season, the team qualified for the Knickerbocker Conference tournament but fell to Dowling, 16–6, in the first round. In 1988, Drew Marino became head coach and posted 25-20 and 14-24 records. The team was led by twins John and Frank Fiorino on the mound, and Frank's ERA was the best in Division II baseball throughout the country.[242] It was during Marino's third year, 1990, that he coached the most successful baseball team in Mercy history.

The 1990 Flyers began their season with a 1-4 stretch in Florida and played slightly better than .500 baseball until the middle of the season, when they began conference play. The team then posted a 17-2 conference record and had a knack for sweeping double-headers with victories against Concordia, Queens and Dowling. The team earned the regular-season conference championship, the first and only in its history. Two of the top three batting averages in a single season occurred in 1990, as Chris Walpole hit .440 and Mitch Trancynenger hit .423.

William Hayward "Mookie" Wilson, who played the majority of his professional baseball career in centerfield with the New York Mets, earned his bachelor's degree from Mercy College in 1996. That same year, he was inducted into the New York Mets Hall of Fame. *Mercy College Library Archives.*

On May 6, the team smashed Dowling, 14–3, in the first round of the Knickerbocker Conference tournament. It was eliminated when it was upset by Concordia, 4–3, two weeks later. The team lost to Sacred Heart and Philadelphia Textile in the ECAC tournament. Head Coach Drew Marino was awarded the title of Knickerbocker Conference Coach of the Year.

The following season would be the last in the Knickerbocker Conference. It was also the last year the team finished with a winning record. The 1991 team finished with a 15-16 record but qualified for the ECAC tournament, losing to Dowling and Adelphi.

The 1995 team featured pitcher and outfielder Brian Sweeney. He was named the NYCAC Scholar Athlete of the Year. Sweeney went on to pitch the second most innings in Mercy history with 224.1 and toss the most complete games with 15. He is the program's all-time strikeout leader with 192. He set the single-season record of 72 strikeouts in 1996. Sweeney made his Major League Baseball debut on August 16, 2003, for the Seattle Mariners. He later pitched for the San Diego Padres and is currently in the Arizona Diamondbacks' system. He has an MLB career total of 117 innings pitched, a 4-2 record and a 3.38 ERA.

In 2000, the team posted a .425 winning percentage at 17-23 under Head Coach Bill Sullivan. In 2007, the team moved to the ECC.

Several Mercy players made the Knickerbocker Conference all-stars, including Steve Buckley, Jerry Meade, Bobby Nigrello, Ed Siller, Chris Walpole and Mike Walpole. All-NYCAC First Team players include Garvin Alston, Anthony Delionado, Bobby Nigrello, Jim Scimone, Mike Walpole and John Weidenhof. Alston was also given all-American honorable mention honors in 1990. Mike Moran was given the NYCAC Rookie of the Year award in 1994. Outfielder Matt Walsh was awarded All-ECC First Team honors in 2009 and earned All-ECC Second Team honors the following two seasons. He was also named to the NCBWA All-East Regional Team in 2009.

Chris Walpole (1987–90) is the all-time leader in hits with 210. Behind him are Matt Walsh (2008–11) with 177 and Rob DiToma (2002–5) with 167. Walpole is second all time in batting average at .374, first in total bases with 320, first in runs with 153, first in RBIs with 123, second in stolen bases with 61, first in doubles with 40, fourth in triples with 9 and fourth in homeruns with 17. His single season batting average of .440 is second all-time. He worked out with the New York Mets in 1995.

One of the most impressive careers in Mercy history belongs to Jim Schult, who played during the 1980–81 seasons. His career batting average is .474, an amazing 100 points ahead of any other Mercy hitter, while his slugging percentage is .820, nearly 160 points ahead of his closest Flyer, John Armento, and his .662 mark in 1989. He also owns the highest on-base percentage of all time at .568. While Schult is not at the top of many career categories since he was a transfer student, his 1981 season is nothing less than spectacular. He recorded 53 hits and set a record with an amazing .541 batting average. He blasted 11 homeruns, a record that was tied by Mike Ewald in 2001. His total bases count of 102 is a record, as is his total runs scored, 55, and slugging percentage, 1.041. His on-base percentage of .640 is 140 points higher than any Mercy baseball player. The Texas Rangers drafted him in 1981.

Matt Foley (2000–3) is the all-time career leader in homeruns with 25. Anthony Delionado (1994–97) is the all-time leader in stolen bases with 87, while John Armento set the single season record of 47 in 1989.

Career leaders in wins for the Mercy pitching staff belong to Ed Siller (1987–90), Dan Bond (1998–2001), Stephen Marsar (2008–11), Garvin Alston (1990–91) and James Scimone (1989–92). Jay Weinberg (1995–98) pitched in the most games with 68 and the most innings with 297.1. Alston has the honor of the program's best ERA with 2.84.[243]

CROSS-COUNTRY/TRACK AND FIELD

The cross-country program, under Head Coach Darryl Bullock, started with five men in the fall of 1976. One year later, the women's program began. Track and field would be offered in the spring for both men and women beginning in 2003. The program ceased after the 2009 season.

Mercy hosted the 2002 NCAA Division II Northeast Regional Cross-Country Championships at Van Cortlandt Park. The team traveled to compete in invitational competitions, and the program often had one of the top GPAs in athletics.

The men's cross-country squad won the inaugural New York Collegiate Athletic Conference championship in 1989. The team qualified to compete in more than twenty NCAA championship competitions, notably a terrific stretch from 2003 to 2008, as the team had "a lot of depth and a real sense of cohesion."[244]

Individuals throughout the years have earned numerous NYCAC and Collegiate Track Conference (CTC) championships. The top men's runner

The 1999 Mercy College cross-country team. *Back row*: Jeremy Schleicher, Irvelt Barolette, Issa Toure, Jessie Tasso, Coach Darryl Bullock, Andrea McGuigan, Paula Gorel and Andrea Lawrence. *Front row*: Capre Arnold, Dale Gearhart and Kristen Perotti. *Courtesy of D. Bullock.*

in the program's history was Damian Williams. The Dublin, Ireland native set the standards for Mercy runners in the late 1980s. He holds most records for the men's program. Other outstanding male runners include Miguel Reyes, John Lucas, Peter Yarema and Jamsel Reyes.

Bullock considers Zoya Pochinka of the Bronx to be the greatest female runner in College history and the "versatile queen of Mercy College track and field."[245] Pochinka, class of 2004, joined the team at thirty-four years old and was a mother of two. In her first race, she broke a Mercy record that had been held for twenty-five years. A week later, she broke it again. In 2002, she set the College's 5K record with a time of 19:54. A year later, she set the indoor mile record with a time of 5:24.1 She was named the 2003–4 NYCAC scholar-athlete and owns every women's record for races over eight hundred meters.[246] Other outstanding Mercy female competitors include Katelyn Klobus and Janet Wong.

The team always considered itself to have a family-like atmosphere. Ironically, the program's first male member, Paul Wood, married the program's first female member, Suzanne Ryan.[247]

Softball

The women of Mercy threw off the mound for the first time in 1978. The team lost its first game to Lehman on April 12, 1978, by a score of 7–4. The team fell to 0-4 before defeating Iona, 17–0, for its first victory in program history. The team concluded the season without losing another game, defeating Pace, Hunter, Marymount and CCNY.

The team managed a 9-3 record during its second season and 13-5 in 1982. The 1984 and 1985 teams were equally impressive, both posting 19-9 records. In 1984, Dayna DeCarlo hit a 3-run homerun to defeat Long Island, 9–8, in the opening round of the state playoffs. Mercy fell to top seed Colgate twice during the following rounds after defeating Canisius. The 1985 team lost to Long Island, 1–0, in its opening game of the New York state playoffs, defeated Pace, 14–6, and then was eliminated by Iona, 5–4.

In 1986, the team put up a 22-10 record. Mercy defeated Niagara twice in the New York State playoffs but fell to Iona twice as well. In 1987, the team put on its best performance with a 22-7 record, a conference title and a New York State Division I-II championship. The team rattled off 9 straight victories near the end of the season, starting with a 7–5 victory over LIU

A 1990s Mercy College girls' softball team in action. *Mercy College Library Archives.*

on April 27. The Flyers defeated Canisius, 10–4, in the state tournament's first round. The team fell to Fairfield to break the streak, 4–3, on May 11 but avenged its loss in a double-header, 6–1, to win the double-elimination tournament and the title.

The team posted a 15-9 mark in 1988 and has failed to have a winning season since. In 2001, 2003 and 2007, the teams went winless. In 2009, the team had its best finish in two decades with a 16-18 record. The following three years, the team has walked the .500 line with finishes of 19-27, 21-23 and 25-26.

Chelsea Methot (2008–11) is the all-time hits leader with 177. Methot is also the all-time leader in homeruns with 34, runs with 110, RBIs with 114, slugging percentage of .676 and total bases with 319.

Dayna DeCarlo owns the all-time leading batting record with a whopping .518 average. She is second all time with 20 homeruns. Jenna Ausiello (2011–12) trails with a .416 average. Auseillo is also the all-time leader in doubles with 35. Regina Barthen (1985–88) is second with a .377 average. Methot ranks third with a .375 average. Ausiello set the all-time mark for single season hits with 67 in 2012.

Paige Cauley (2009–11) finished her career with a .341 batting average and fourth all time in hits with 124. She is second all time in runs with 87, second in RBIs with 69, second in all-time bases with 198, third in doubles with 30 and third in homeruns with 14.

Jean Gutierrez (1988–90) has the most stolen bases in Mercy history with 31 and finished her career only being thrown out once. She is also the all-time leader in walks.

DeCarlo set the single season batting average in 1984 with a whopping .530. Caitlin Kruger challenged the mark in 2004 by batting .491. She moved into second place, past the mark of DeCarlo, who batted .484 in 1981 during her freshman year.

Julie Doering (1987–88) earned the most career wins for a Mercy pitcher with 28. Mary Sieber (2011–active) is second with 20 wins. Jean Sanborn collected 19 wins from the 1989 to 1992 seasons, third all time.

Kellie Quinn (1995–98) has started the most games with 73 and made the most appearances with 88. Quinn owns records for most innings pitched (425) and most complete games (64).

Stephanie Pereyo (2007–9) recorded the most career strikeouts with 172. In 2012, freshman Alexandra Puglisi recorded 160 strikeouts to shatter the single-season record and vault her into second place all time. Quinn ranks third with 158 strikeouts, while Sieber is fourth with 131. Puglisi is now first all time in career ERA at 2.05, breaking Doering's mark of 2.27. Puglisi owns the single-season record mark of 15 wins, also breaking Doering's record of 14, which she did in the 1987 and 1988 seasons. Lori Roemer posted the best single-season ERA of 1.56 in 1987, followed by Jean Sanborn's 1.65 in 1989.[248]

Men's Soccer

Based on winning percentage, the men's soccer team has been the most successful and consistent in Mercy history, finishing with winning seasons in nine of its first ten seasons and eighteen out of thirty-one.

The team debuted in 1979. In 1981, the team finished with a respectable 10-6-5 record and repeated a 10-win performance the following season. Yet it was not until 1986 that the team recorded its best season in Mercy history with a 15-4-1 record behind sweeper Paul Woodley. After three 1-goal losses, the team sat at 2-3. It then rattled off 7 straight wins against the likes of Pace,

NY Tech and Concordia. After a stumble against Monmouth, the team won another 7 straight games against Bridgeport, C.W. Post and King's College. The season ended with a 1–1 tie against Brooklyn. The team earned a share of the Suburban Conference title and a top-twenty Division II ranking.

The program continued its momentum with a 13-6-3 campaign with notable victories against Monmouth, Concordia and Bridgeport. Mercy was ranked among the top twenty Division II schools in the country for the second year in a row, led by Mercy Hall of Fame goalie Andrew McGovern, and was runner up in the ECAC championship to Keene State University. The team won 10 games in 1988. In 1989, it had a 12-2-3 season. The Flyers advanced to the NCAA regional finals and made history by winning the first-ever NYCAC conference title. First-year coach David Symes was awarded NYCAC Coach of the Year honors, and the team finished ranked seventh in Division II nationally.[249]

A few seasons later, the team registered thirteen-win seasons during three consecutive seasons from 1992 to 1994. The 1992 team won the NYCAC crown but lost in the ECAC tournament finals to Concordia, 1–0. The 1993 team took second in the NYCAC yet won the ECAC tournament with a 3–1 victory over South Hampton and a 5–1 victory against NYIT.[250]

The 1998 team posted a 13-7-1 record, and the 2004 team posted a successful 12-6-1 campaign. In 2012, the men's soccer team posted a 10-5-3 record and advanced to the ECC tournament's semifinals, losing to eventual champion C.W. Post. Senior William Koki was named to the Daktronics NCAA Division II All-East Region Second Team and All-ECC first team.

Dennis Prince (1985–88) is Mercy's all-time leading scorer with 44 goals. He is also the all-time leader in total points (113) and assists. He set the single-season record for goals in a season (22) and total points (57) in 1986.

Robert Rennis (2002–4) is second all time in career goals with 32. Behind him is Vance Waul (1992–94) with 28. Tied for fourth place are Albert Abaidoo (1998–99) and Morris Cyrus (1990–93) with 25 each.

Andrew McGovern (1987–89) is the all-time leader in saves with 214. He is also the career leader in shutouts with 15. Jose Figueroa (2000–2002) is second all time in saves with 182. He has the highest career save percentage with .71.[251]

Women's Volleyball

The women's volleyball program held its initial game on September 23, 1980, and earned a victory against St. Francis, 3–0. After dropping three straight games to fall to a 2-5 record, the team went on a miraculous run to close the season out with 11 straight victories, sweeping Nyack, 3–0, in the final game of the year, to go 13-5 and win the Hudson Valley Women's Athletic Conference title under coaches Victor and Elaine Pagano.

In 1981, the team ironically finished the season winning its last 11 games again. The team finished 23-5 and lost only two sets against New Rochelle in its final 9 games. Mercy continued its momentum in 1982 and registered a 16-5 record. Just like its predecessors, the team finished the season with a 6-game winning streak. The team finished 19-11-1 in 1983, 11-7-1 in 1984 and 16-10 in 1985. The team had its first losing season in 1986 with a 5-18 record.

The team had stellar numbers throughout the 1990s, including records of 31-12, 26-12 and 31-13 from 1992 to 1994. The most successful regular season was 1999, when the team registered a tremendous 37-4 record. It also began a string of three consecutive NYCAC conference championships. The team won its first 21 games until it fell, 3–2, to the University of Puerto Rico–Bayaman. Mercy advanced to the NCAA tournament regionals, losing to Pace, 15–12, 8–15, 18–16 and 15–6.

The team roared back with an outstanding 33-2 record in the 2000 season. Mercy won in the NCAA regionals against Queens College, 8–15, 15–12, 15–9 and 15–11. Mercy was eliminated by Pace again, this time in the Northeast Regional Championship, 15–12, 3–15, 15–8, 8–15 and 15–11.

The team posted a 34-2 record in 2001 and advanced the deepest in the NCAA tournament in College history. Mercy lost its opening set to Bryant in the regionals, 34–32. The team won the next three sets, all by scores of 30–18. Mercy then swept Queens College, 32–30, 30–25 and 32–30 in the Northeast Regional Championship. Mercy won the first set in the Elite Eight against Grand Valley State but lost a tense best of five series, 25–30, 30–26, 30–19, 28–30 and 15–9. Yulissa Zamudio was named to the tournament's first team by finishing with 37 kills and 36 digs. She led the tournament with a .413 average.[252]

There have been many successful Mercy volleyball players. Zamudio was named NYCAC Player of the Year. Garvey Pierre was awarded NYCAC Coach of the Year. Zamudio, Monica Herrera, Adreann Stevens and Marie France Jean-Francois were All-Conference selections. Debra Waite (1992–95) is the current all-time leader in kills with 1,654. Waite would be a four-time NYCAC first-conference selection. Katiana Dorfleus (2002–5) is second in kills with 1,525. Zamudio (2001–3) is third with 1,515. Orita Stewart (1995–98) is fourth with 1,456, and Monica Herrera (2000–2001, 2005) is fifth with 1,380. Herrera is also the all-time leader in aces with 350. Winy Fred Victor (1997–2000) is the all-time assist leader with 4,519. Second is Jennifer Hunter (1991–94). Hunter also is the all-time leader in matches (156) and games (549) played. In third for assists is Simone Forbes (2002–5) with 2,440. Paula Williams (1991–94) is the all-time leader in digs with 1,717. Waite is second with 1,525. Waite is also the career leader in blocks with 786. Single-season leaders are Orita Stewart (1997) with 688 kills, Winy Fred Victor (1999) with 1,489 assists, Paula Williams (1991) with 662 digs and Heather O'Leary (1993) with 315 blocked shots.[253]

In 2011, Brenna White set the Mercy freshman record for kills and led all NCAA divisions with 652 kills. It was the second-best single-season mark in Mercy history. She was named ECC Rookie of the Week and to the ECC Player of the Week Honor Roll multiple times.[254]

Men's Tennis

The inaugural match for the men's tennis team was against Stony Brook in 1981, in which Mercy lost, 6.5–2.5. Mercy rebounded in an impressive fashion, registering its first winning streak: a 6–3 victory over Bridgeport and an 8–1 victory over Manhattan. After playing slightly above .500 tennis midway through the season, the Flyers won their next six games to finish the season with wins over Lehman, Nyack, USMMA, NYIT, Maritime, Adelphi and NYU. In 1982, a squad consisting of Neil Keating, Jimmy Morgan White, Andy Broderick and John Boccari posted a 10-5 record and won the Region Co-Championship.[255]

Scarce records exist of all tennis matches, yet records show that the tennis team recorded winning or greater than .500 teams until the 1984 season. The team regained steam during the 1987 season with a 7-2 record. However, the best was saved for the 1989 season. The team finished a perfect 13-0 under Head Coach Jim Thompson and won the Suburban Division of the Metropolitan Tennis Conference. The team took that success into the next season, winning its first 6 games. It set a Mercy tennis record by winning 19 straight games, a streak finally halted by NY Tech. In 1990, the team finished with only 2 losses as Dean Evanson made it to the NYCAC Single's

Tournament finals.[256] "The players were very special in this program. I told them to be great students, great tennis players, and great citizens. And they obliged," said Thompson.[257]

The team also registered impressive records in its final seasons. During the 2005 season, the team posted a 10-4 record before falling to Assumption in the first round of the NCAA tournament. During its final season, the team posted an 8-2 regular season record before defeating Dowling in the ECC semifinals, 5–3, and losing to Concordia, 5–0, in the ECC finals. Mercy defeated Queens, 5–1, in the NCAA tournament's first round and then impressively defeated Kutztown, 5–3, in the tournament's second round. The final match in men's tennis history was a loss to Armstrong Atlantic State on May 9, 2009, by a score of 5–1.[258]

Men's Golf

The men's golf team teed off for its first match on April 6, 1981, under Head Coach Tony Macellaro. The team shot a 372 in a dual meet against Wagner and Rutgers. The team hovered around that mark for most of the year but had its best showing in the MGA tournament by shooting a 284. In 1983, the team traveled to Yale and placed fifth in a ten-team tournament. The team competed against teams like Seton Hall, Fordham, Hofstra, Pace and Iona over the next decade.

The team played the NYCAC tournament in the 1990 season. Mercy won four of the first five conference titles. After winning the initial title, Pace won in year two, and then Mercy won three in a row behind Steve Vasquez, Rick Paladino, Dwayne Powell, John Cipolla and Andy Lehman.[259]

Mercy won consecutive conference titles in 1999 and 2000, led by Clayton Johnson, class of 2001. He was inducted into the Mercy Hall of Fame in 2011. In 1999, Johnson's round of 76 at the Ardsley Country Club earned him medalist honors, as he was the only athlete to shoot under 80. A year later, heavy rain, hail and winds did not stop him from shooting a low 76 at the eighteen-hole Qualifying Round of the 51st Metropolitan Golf Association Intercollegiate Division I Championship against the likes of Rutgers, St. John's, Columbia, Fairfield, Hofstra, Army, Rider and Fordham. He then shot 77 and 79 in the thirty-six-hole MGA Division I Tournament, held at the St. Andrew's Golf Club in Hastings. He tied for thirteenth and was the only Division II athlete to place in the top fifty.

The team's best two scores occurred in the 1989 season, an astounding 173 in a dual meet against Hofstra and NYIT on April 18, 1989. The squad also shot a 241 against MGA. The 1987 team shot a 243 against MGA. The 1983 team shot 249 against Adelphi. The 1992 team shot a 252 in a dual meet against Queens and Dowling.

In 2001, the team placed second in the NYCAC. The team disbanded in 2002, shooting its last match against Adelphi.[260]

WOMEN'S SOCCER

The women's soccer team's first season occurred in 2000 under Head Coach Melissa Mann. The team played its first match on September 12 and lost to C.W. Post, 14–0. On September 25, the team earned its first victory over NJIT, 2–1. In 2001, the team posted a 5-10-1 record, its best overall record to date. The team won matchups against NJIT, Concordia, NYIT, Queens and Molloy.

Kristin Hunt (2001–2) has the most career goals for Mercy with 15. Avaleen Blake (2000–2003) and Lindsay Levasseur (2003–6) trail her with 8. Hunt set the single-season mark for goals with 10 in 2001. Hunt also is the career leader in total points with 33. Michelle Bernal (2000–2003) is in second place with 25. Goalkeeper Lesly Moonsalve (2001–3) is the career leader in total saves (460), career save percentage (.727) and career shutouts (3).[261]

LACROSSE

Mercy launched its men's and women's lacrosse programs in 2010. The men's team played its first game on February 28 on the road against American International. Frank Henenlotter assisted classmate Mike Marzocca for the extra-man goal and the program's first score. The Mavericks won the game, 6–5. The team played its first home game a week later against Pace in a losing effort, 4–3. The team lost six games in a row before splitting its final eight games and finishing 5-10.

The inaugural season was certainly not an indication of seasons to come; the team grew by leaps and bounds in its second season and posted an

11-3 record and a 7-3 conference record. The team won its opener, 7–6, against Mount St. Alselm and then won four in a row in impressive fashion. The team was ranked no. 8 in the USILA Coaches Poll. In an anticipated matchup, the team fell to no. 6 Mercyhurst, 9–7. After beating Molloy, 8–4, Mercy rose to no. 6 in the rankings.

A showdown against no. 2 C.W. Post earned national attention in the lacrosse world. Mercy fell behind 8–1 but rallied back, giving the defending champions a scare. Post won, 15–12. Post finished the season no. 1 in the polls.

Mercy remained at no. 6 in the polls and lost a hard-fought battle to no. 7 Dowling, 11–5, to wrap its season. Mercy finished no. 7. Head Coach Steve Manitta was named ECC Coach of the Year. Goalkeeper T.J. DiCarlo was named the Division II Goalkeeper of the Year and First Team All-American. He recorded 180 saves and a 7.58 goals against average and totaled a save percentage of .636.

The 2012 team struggled within its extremely competitive conference, posting a 6-7 overall record and a 4-6 conference record. Marzocca scored 32 points and had 10 assists. After scoring 5 goals in a 12–11 victory over Molloy, he was named the Nike Men's Lacrosse Player of the Week on April 9, 2012. He also won ECC Player of the Week for consecutive weeks in April.[262]

A week after the men began their 2010 season, the women took the field at Manhattanville and won, 16–9, in their program's debut under Head Coach Francesca DeLorenzo. Marissa Hurley scored the first goal in Maverick history, as she and Jamie McPartland both scored 4 goals in their debut. The team would finish 8-6 and 3-4 in the conference.

For a program to finish with a winning record was a tremendous feat for the team. Three women received Second Team All-ECC honors: Brianne Horn, who led the team with 43 goals; Kelsey Sullivan, who led the team in assists, groundballs, ball controls and forced turnovers; and McPartland, who was third on the team in goals and points.

In 2011, the team posted a 9-6 overall record with a 5-3 conference record after battling inclement weather all season. After losing to no. 8 C.W. Post, the team finished the season with a 2-game winning streak over Lake Erie and Seton Hill. Sullivan again was named Second Team All-ECC and led the team in points with 49.

The 2012 team posted a 7-8 season with a 4-4 conference record. The team started a shocking 0-5, defeated Chestnut Hill, 16–7, and then lost its next 2 games to fall to 1-7. The team won its next 5 games against Kutztown, Seton Hill, Lake Erie, Assumption and St. Thomas Aquinas.

The team won its last game of the season with a season-high 19 goals against Bridgeport. In that game, Hurley became the first Mercy lacrosse player to reach 100 goals. Goalkeeper Stephanie DiLegge was named to the All-ECC First Team. She led all of Division I and II lacrosse with a .558 save percentage. She recorded 172 saves.[263]

Field Hockey

The women's field hockey team began during the 2010 season under Head Coach Kayte Kinsley. The first game in program history was a loss, at Limestone, 5–0, on September 4, 2010. The program's first goal came on September 17 against Thomas College (Maine), scored by freshman Kristen Sliman. The team finished with a 0-13 record. The program's first win came the following season on October 7, 2011, on the road against Elms College. Giana Magosin scored 2 goals in the win. The team finished 1-15. Goalkeeper Kristen Znaniecki led Division II with 11.09 saves per game. In three seasons, Znaniecki posted 408 saves.

The 2012 team posted a 2-15 record, with wins over Richard Stockton and Daniel Webster. Marissa Kluber led the team in goals (4) and points (9). Sophomore Danielle Jones was elected to the ISA All-Conference team. She finished the season with 2 goals and 9 defensive saves.[264]

Hall of Fame

Mercy unveiled its Hall of Fame in 2006. Every member has his or her name enshrined in the athletic hallway in Main Hall. In 2006, the inaugural inductees included Stacy Gillespie, women's basketball ('88); Neil Judge, athletic director/coach; Carol Schachner-Leib, women's basketball coach; James Schult, baseball ('84); and Paul Woodley, men's soccer ('90). The second class, inducted in 2008, included Robert Davis, men's basketball ('86); Dayna DeCarlo, softball ('85); Pat Geoghegan, baseball ('83); Andrew McGovern, men's soccer ('90); Rick Wolff, baseball coach; and the 2001 women's volleyball team. The 2009 class included Mary Brechbiel Agnetti, women's basketball ('78); Noreen Annunziata, women's basketball ('86); Bob Crescenzo, baseball ('82); and Brian Donohue, men's basketball ('78). In

2011, Mercy inducted its fourth class: Chris Walpole, baseball ('90); Clayton Johnson, golf ('01); Tom Sivulich, men's basketball ('80); Debra Waite Connery Smith, volleyball ('96); and the 1975–76 women's basketball team. The 2012 class consisted of Eleni Kousoulas Pallogudis, softball ('90); Brian Sweeney, baseball ('07); Tony Macellaro, men's golf coach; the 1989 men's soccer team; and the 1961–65 women's basketball teams.[265]

Afterword

From the day the Sisters of Mercy founded Mercy College, students, faculty, staff, alumni and friends have held a shared commitment to student success, innovation and service to others. These important attributes have been proudly and emphatically upheld throughout the College's history. With dedicated and enthusiastic leaders at the helm, Mercy College has made tremendous progress since our founders forged their initial path.

In every corner of this College, motivated students thrive to learn, grow and make a difference in their lives and the lives of future generations. While embracing the pursuit of knowledge, dedicated faculty members are committed to inspiring and academically empowering our students to reach their greatest potential. The dedicated staff ensures that Mercy's mission is carried forth, helping to transform lives with personalized attention.

Our strength lies in our commitment to making students our first priority, imparting excellence in the classrooms coupled with support and resources, as well as mentoring and skills building, career services and leadership development.

As the current-day stewards carrying on our founders' dreams, we now set our aspirations beyond the horizon, challenging ourselves to improve every aspect of the College with insightful, bold planning and disciplined, confident execution.

As the College continues to grow to a position of national prominence, we look to the future with the same resolve once intended by our founders. It is with the same spirit of innovation, commitment to student success, academic excellence and engagement with our community that Mercy College will continue to provide a quality, affordable education, ensuring that our graduates leave with the skill set, intellectual curiosity and knowledge base to succeed in today's world.

Dr. Kimberly R. Cline
President, Mercy College (2008–present)

Notes

Chapter 1

1. "Alma Mater" was written by Donald Sivack and adapted to Handel's music by John Rayburn. Both were Mercy College professors. See Sister Mary Agnes Parrell, *The History of Mercy College, 1950–1982* (Dobbs Ferry, NY: Mercy College, 1985), 6–7, 16, 19.
2. Ibid., 2.
3. *Engage: The Magazine from Mercy College* 1, "A New College's First President" (Summer/Fall 2007): 2.
4. Sister Mary Joannes Christie, dedication of Sister Mary Gratia Maher Hall, May 5, 1982, in Parrell, *History of Mercy College*, 65–67.
5. Commencement Exercises Program, 1970, in Parrell, *History of Mercy College*, 14.
6. Mary Neumann, *The Letters of Catherine McAuley* (Westminster, MD: Helicon, 1969); Sister Mary Sullivan, *Catherine McAuley and the Tradition of Mercy* (Notre Dame, IN: University of Notre Dame Press, 1995); Sister M. Bertrand Degnan, *Mercy Unto Thousands: The Life of Mother Catherine McAuley* (Westminster, MD: Newman, 1957); M. Angela Bolster, *Catherine McAuley: Her Educational Thought and Its Influence on the Origins and Development of an Irish Training College* (Dublin, Ireland: Our Lady of Mercy College, 1981).
7. Maureen Fitzgerald, "Habits of Compassion: Irish American Nuns in New York City," *Women's America: Refocusing the Past*, eds. Linda Kerber, Jane Sherron De Hart and Cornelia Hughes Dayton, 7th ed. (New York: Oxford University Press, 2011); Kathleen Healy, *Frances Warde: American Founder of the Sisters of Mercy* (New York: Seabury, 1973); Karen Kennelly, ed., *American Catholic Women: A Historical Exploration* (New York: Macmillan, 1989); Austin Carroll, *Leaves from the Annals of the Sisters of Mercy*, 3 vols. (New York: Catholic Publication Society, 1889).
8. By 1860, the Irish composed 1.6 of the 2.2 million Catholics in America. Between 1830 and 1900, Catholic women formed 106 new foundations of women religious, eventually composing a collective workforce of about fifty thousand people. Kerby Miller, *Emigrants and Exiles: Ireland and the Irish Exodus to North America* (New York: Oxford University Press, 1985); William Shannon, *The American Irish* (New York: Collier, 1963); Hasia Diner, *Erin's Daughters in America: Irish Immigrant Women in the Nineteenth Century* (Baltimore, MD: Johns Hopkins University Press, 1983).

9. Sister Mary Jeremy Daigler, *Through the Windows: A History of the Work of Higher Education Among the Sisters of Mercy of the Americas* (Scranton, PA: University of Scranton Press, 2001), 1–2.
10. Kathleen Mahoney, *Catholic Higher Education in Protestant America: The Jesuits and Harvard in the Age of the University* (Baltimore, MD: Johns Hopkins University Press, 2003).
11. Margaret Vetare, *Philipsburg Manor Upper Mills* (Pocantico Hills, NY: Historic Hudson Valley Press, 2004), 18–22; Edgar Mayhew Bacon, *Chronicles of Tarrytown and Sleepy Hollow* (New York: G.P. Putnam's Sons, 1897); Katherine Burton, *His Mercy Endureth Forever* (Tarrytown, NY: Sisters of Mercy, 1946).
12. Sister Mary Gertrude to John D. Rockefeller Jr., Folder 232, Box 35, Educational Interests series, Record Group 2, Office of the Messiers Rockefeller (OMR), Rockefeller Family Archives, Rockefeller Archive Center, Sleepy Hollow, New York (hereafter designated RAC).
13. Parrell, *History of Mercy College*, 6.
14. Daigler, *Through the Windows*, 131; interview with Dr. Ann Grow, Irvington, New York, October 24, 2012; Sister Mary Gratia Maher, *The Organization of Religious Instruction in Catholic Colleges for Women* (Washington, D.C.: Catholic University of America Press, 1951).
15. Parrell, *History of Mercy College*, 2; Daigler, *Through the Windows*, 132.
16. Parrell, *History of Mercy College*, 3–4, 7.
17. Ibid., 4.
18. Dana Creel to Nelson Rockefeller, February 8, 1956, Folder 233, Box 35, Educational Interests series, RG 2, OMR, Rockefeller Family Archives, RAC.
19. William Yates to John D. Rockefeller Jr., November 19, 1956, Folder 233, Box 35, Educational Interests series, RG 2, OMR, Rockefeller Family Archives, RAC.
20. Mother Mary Jeanne Ferrier to John D. Rockefeller Jr., March 25, 1958, Folder 233, Box 35, Educational Interests series, RG 2, OMR, Rockefeller Family Archives, RAC.
21. Mother Mary Jeanne Ferrier to William Yates, December 4, 1956, Folder 233, Box 35, Educational Interests series, RG 2, OMR, Rockefeller Family Archives, RAC; William Yates to John D. Rockefeller Jr., October 22, 1956, Folder 233, Box 35, Educational Interests series, RG 2, OMR, Rockefeller Family Archives, RAC; William Yates to John D. Rockefeller Jr., May 23, 1957, Folder 233, Box 35, Educational Interests series, RG 2, OMR, Rockefeller Family Archives, RAC.
22. William Yates to John D. Rockefeller Jr., February 15, 1956, Folder 233, Box 35, Educational Interests series, RG 2, OMR, Rockefeller Family Archives, RAC; William Yates to John D. Rockefeller Jr., March 3, 1956, Folder 233, Box 35, Educational Interests series, RG 2, OMR, Rockefeller Family Archives, RAC; William Yates to John D. Rockefeller Jr., October 22, 1956, Folder 233, Box 35, Educational Interests series, RG 2, OMR, Rockefeller Family Archives, RAC; letter from John D. Rockefeller Jr., October 24, 1956, Folder 233, Box 35, Educational Interests series, RG 2, OMR, Rockefeller Family Archives, RAC.
23. William Yates to John D. Rockefeller Jr., July 15, 1957, Folder 233, Box 35, Educational Interests series, RG 2, OMR, Rockefeller Family Archives, RAC.
24. Philip Keebler to John D. Rockefeller Jr., April 8, 1958, Folder 233, Box 35, Educational Interests series, RG 2, OMR, Rockefeller Family Archives, RAC; William Yates to Philip Keebler, March 28, 1958, Folder 233, Box 35, Educational Interests series, RG 2, OMR, Rockefeller Family Archives, RAC.
25. Mother Mary Jeanne Ferrier to John D. Rockefeller Jr., March 25, 1958, Folder 233, Box 35, Educational Interests series, RG 2, OMR, Rockefeller Family Archives, RAC.

26. John D. Rockefeller Jr. to Mother Mary Jeanne Ferrier, April 8, 1958, Folder 233, Box 35, Educational Interests series, RG 2, OMR, Rockefeller Family Archives, RAC.
27. *New York Times*, June 23, 1958.
28. Memorandum to Mother Mary Jeanne Ferrier, July 6, 1959, Folder 234, Box 35, Educational Interests series, RG 2, OMR, Rockefeller Family Archives, RAC; memorandum to Philip Keebler, August 19, 1958, Folder 233, Box 35, Educational Interests series, RG 2, OMR, Rockefeller Family Archives, RAC.
29. Parrell, *History of Mercy College*, 4; William Yates to Paul Folwell, August 6, 1958, Folder 233, Box 35, Educational Interests series, RG 2, OMR, Rockefeller Family Archives, RAC.
30. Philip Keebler to William Yates, July 22, 1958, Folder 233, Box 35, Educational Interests series, RG 2, OMR, Rockefeller Family Archives, RAC.
31. The event received wide media coverage. *Catholic News*, October 25, 1958; *New York Times*, October 22, 1958; *Tarrytown Daily News*, October 21, 1958.
32. *New York Times*, May 21, 1962.
33. *Tarrytown Daily News*, October 21, 1958.
34. The transcript is contained in Folder 234, Box 35, Educational Interests series, RG 2, OMR, Rockefeller Family Archives, RAC.
35. Philip Keebler to Robert Gumbel, September 4, 1958, Folder 233, Box 35, Educational Interests series, RG 2, OMR, Rockefeller Family Archives, RAC; Philip Keebler to William Sanders, September 4, 1958, Folder 233, Box 35, Educational Interests series, RG 2, OMR, Rockefeller Family Archives, RAC.
36. Vera Goeller to Sister Mary Brendon, December 18, 1958, Folder 233, Box 35, Educational Interests series, RG 2, OMR, Rockefeller Family Archives, RAC.
37. Philip Keebler to John D. Rockefeller Jr., January 5, 1960, Folder 233, Box 35, Educational Interests series, RG 2, OMR, Rockefeller Family Archives, RAC.
38. *New York Times*, December 13, 1959.
39. Malcolm Wilson, commencement address, January 1982, in Parrell, *History of Mercy College*, 65.
40. John D. Rockefeller Jr. to William Yates, March 13, 1958, Folder 233, Box 35, Educational Interests series, RG 2, OMR, Rockefeller Family Archives, RAC; William Yates to John D. Rockefeller Jr., October 22, 1956, Folder 233, Box 35, Educational Interests series, RG 2, OMR, Rockefeller Family Archives, RAC.
41. Mother Mary Jeanne Ferrier to John D. Rockefeller Jr., June 28, 1959, Folder 234, Box 35, Educational Interests series, RG 2, OMR, Rockefeller Family Archives, RAC.
42. Mother Mary Jeanne to John D. Rockefeller Jr., 1960, Folder 233, Box 35, Educational Interests series, RG 2, OMR, Rockefeller Family Archives, RAC.
43. Sister Mary Agnes Parrell and James Neal, "Mercy College on Historic Wickers Creek," *Wickers Creek: An Interdisciplinary Review* 1 (1983): 1–5; Parrell, *History of Mercy College*, 21–22.
44. Mary Sudman Donovan, *George Washington at "Head Quarters, Dobbs Ferry"* (New York: iUniverse, 2009); Eric Martone, "Comte de Rochambeau," *International Encyclopedia of Protest and Revolution*, ed. Immanuel Ness (Malden, MA: Blackwell, 2009).
45. Sister Mary Agnes Parrell, *Profiles of Dobbs Ferry* (Dobbs Ferry, NY: Oceana Publications, 1976), 35–36.
46. *New York Times*, February 26, 1917.
47. See his obituary in the *New York Times*, July 13, 1933.
48. *Time*, July 31, 1933.

49. Elaine Marranzano, "'Mansions' Return to Tarrytown's Wilson Park," *Tarrytown-Sleepy Hollow Patch*, July 26, 2011. http://tarrytown.patch.com/articles/mansions-return-to-tarrytowns-wilson-park-but-pale-in-comparison-to-majestic-estates-of-past.
50. *New York Times*, May 21, 1962; Parrell, *History of Mercy College*, 6, 8.
51. Daigler, *Through the Windows*, 132.
52. *New York Times*, May 21, 1962; Parrell, *History of Mercy College*, 8.
53. Mercy College Annual Report, 2008, 13, Mercy College Library Archives, Dobbs Ferry, New York (hereafter designated MCLA).
54. *New York Times*, December 19, 1964; Parrell, *History of Mercy College*, 8, 14; Mercy College Self-Evaluation Report, 1966–67, MCLA.
55. Parrell, *History of Mercy College*, 7, 10–11; Self-Evaluation Report, 1966–67, MCLA.
56. Parrell, *History of Mercy College*, 9–10.
57. Ibid., 9, 11.
58. Ibid., 8–9, 12.
59. Annual Report, 2008, MCLA, 13; Parrell, *History of Mercy College*, 7.
60. Quoted in Parrell, *History of Mercy College*, 60
61. Christie, dedication of Maher Hall, in Parrell, *History of Mercy College*, 66; Parrell, *History of Mercy College*, 12; on the lone male student, see Self-Evaluation Report, 1966–67, MCLA, 88.
62. William Farrell, "21 Colleges Ruled Ineligible for Aid," *New York Times*, January 6, 1970.
63. Daigler, *Through the Windows*, 136.
64. Letter from Sister Mary Etheldreda Christie to Edward Nyquist, May 4, 1969, Sisters of Mercy Archives, Hartsdale, New York, in Daigler, *Through the Windows*, 134.
65. Interview between Daigler and Agnes O'Grady, Mercy College treasurer from 1961 to 1969, Bronx, New York, March 6, 1997, in Daigler, *Through the Windows*, 133.
66. Malcolm Wilson, commencement address, January 1982, in Parrell, *History of Mercy College*, 65.
67. Parrell, *History of Mercy College*, 12–13.
68. Sisters of Mercy Archives in Daigler, *Through the Windows*, 133, 134–35.
69. Interview with Grow, October 24, 2012.
70. Parrell, *History of Mercy College*, 13–14.
71. Robert McCooey, commencement address, summer 1972, in Parrell, *History of Mercy College*, 17–18.
72. Parrell, *History of Mercy College*, 16, 18, 22.
73. Ibid., 9.

Chapter 2

74. See Dr. Donald Grunewald's Linkedin profile at www.linkedin.com/pub/donald-grunewald/13/ab9/8bb.
5. Parrell, *History of Mercy College*, 19.
76. Phone interview with Dr. Donald Grunewald, September 24, 2012.
77. Lena Williams, "Mercy's President Leaves His Calling," *New York Times*, August 26, 1984; Gary Kriss, "Grunewald to Focus on Museum Funds," *New York Times*, May 19, 1985.
78. Parrell, *History of Mercy College*, 19, 69.

79. Williams, "Mercy's President"; interview with Grunewald, September 24, 2012; interview with Grow, October 24, 2012.
80. Parrell, *History of Mercy College*, 22–23, 33, 47.
81. Interview with Grunewald, September 24, 2012.
82. Draft Report to the Middle States Commission on Higher Education, 2003, MCLA, 6; Donald Grunewald, "Are Costs Foreclosing Opportunity for Higher Education?" *New York Times*, July 24, 1977; Williams, "Mercy's President"; Jill Silverman, "Colleges Compete for Adults," *New York Times*, December 7, 1980; Lena Williams, "A Fast-Growing College and Its Critics," *New York Times*, March 20, 1980; Parrell, *History of Mercy College*, 23, 33; interview with Grunewald, September 24, 2012.
83. Interview with Grunewald, September 24, 2012; Ronald Smothers, "College Mergers: Marriage of Convenience," *New York Times*, April 23, 1978.
84. *Engage: The Magazine for Mercy College* 2, "The Age of Expansion" (Winter/Spring 2008): 2.
85. Interview with Grow, October 24, 2012.
86. Williams, "Fast-Growing College."
87. Ibid.
88. Parrell, *History of Mercy College*, 32–33, 35–36, 40–41, 67–69; Mercy College Annual Report, 1990–91, MCLA; interview with Grow, October 24, 2012.
89. Parrell, *History of Mercy College*, 27, 36.
90. Michael Mooney, memorandum, in Parrell, *History of Mercy College*, 67; Progress Report of Mercy College, 1982, MCLA, 13.
91. Parrell, *History of Mercy College*, 35, 58, 68.
92. Luisa Kreisberg, "Mercy College Brings Classes to the County Shopping Center—and the People," *New York Times*, February 20, 1977; Williams, "Fast-Growing College"; Parrell, *History of Mercy College*, 35.
93. Parrell, *History of Mercy College*, 32, 36, 38, 41–43, 49, 57.
94. Ibid., 26, 42.
95. Interview with Grunewald, September 24, 2012; Parrell, *History of Mercy College*, 25.
96. Meeting Book, 1974–75, in Parrell, *History of Mercy College*, 25; meeting of the board of trustees, May 12, 1975, in Parrell, *History of Mercy College*, 28.
97. Parrell, *History of Mercy College*, 35–36, 59.
98. Christie, dedication of Maher Hall, in Parrell, *History of Mercy College*, 65–67; Progress Report of Mercy College, 1982, MCLA, 9.
99. Parrell, *History of Mercy College*, 28, 39, 46–47; board of trustees meeting, March 4, 1978, in Parrell, *History of Mercy College*, 42; E. Kappy, "The New Look," *Mercy at the Moment*, October 1978; interview with Grunewald, September 24, 2012.
100. Parrell, *History of Mercy College*, 28.
101. Ibid., 16–17, 21, 25, 29, 32, 38–39, 46, 59–60, 63.
102. Richard Stevenson, "Finding and Marketing that Something Special," *New York Times*, January 5, 1986; Smothers, "College Mergers"; Progress Report of Mercy College, 1982, MCLA, 17–18.
103. Parrell, *History of Mercy College*, 22, 26, 37, 48, 54; interview with Grunewald, September 24, 2012; Merri Rosenburg, "LIU Chooses Space at Purchase," *New York Times*, April 2, 2000.
104. George Goodman Jr., "White Harlem Dentist to Teach Black Studies," *New York Times*, September 11, 1972; Kreisberg, "Mercy College Brings Classes."

105. Parrell, *History of Mercy College*, 22–23, 34, 36–37, 52; Williams, "Mercy's President"; Progress Report of Mercy College, 1982, MCLA, 10; interview with Grunewald, September 24, 2012.
106. *New York Times*, August 8, 1984.
107. Mercy College Annual Report, 2008, MCLA, 13; Williams, "Fast-Growing College"; Edward Hudson, "Campuses Humming into the Night," *New York Times*, August 28, 1977.
108. Parrell, *History of Mercy College*, 31–33, 35, 38, 53; interview with Grunewald, September 24, 2012.
109. Parrell, *History of Mercy College*, 52; interview with Grunewald, September 24, 2012.
110. Williams, "Mercy's President."
111. Williams, "Fast-Growing College."
112. Williams, "Mercy's President."
113. Rhoda Gilinsky, "Ethics Institute Set Up at Mercy College," *New York Times*, September 20, 1978; Rhoda Gilinsky, "Centers for Peace Find Homes in the County," *New York Times*, November 18, 1984; Rhoda Gilinsky, "County Celebrates UN Anniversary," *New York Times*, October 20, 1985; Parrell, *History of Mercy College*, 53.
114. Meeting of the Executive Committee of the International Association of University Presidents, June 1979, in Parrell, *History of Mercy College*, 52.
115. Parrell, *History of Mercy College*, 43–45, 50–52; Progress Report of Mercy College, 1982, MCLA, 20.
116. Parrell, *History of Mercy College*, 19, 58–59, 63.
117. Bridget Paolucci, "College Searches for Italian Heritage," *New York Times*, September 11, 1977; Betsy Brown, "The 'Italianization' of Dobbs Ferry," *New York Times*, September 27, 1981.
118. Parrell, *History of Mercy College*, 31, 38.
119. Paolucci, "College Searches for Italian Heritage"; Parrell, *History of Mercy College*, 46, 53, 60; Joseph Sciorra, "*Ricorso* and *Rinascita* in the Twenty-first Century," *Italian-American Review* 1 (Winter 2011): v–vi.
120. Parrell, *History of Mercy College*, 38; Donald Grunewald, memorandum to Mercy College Community, January 18, 1980, in Parrell, *History of Mercy College*, 56–57; Progress Report of Mercy College, 1982, MCLA, 19.
121. Program for commencement exercises, May 24, 1972, in Parrell, *History of Mercy College*, 17
122. Letter from Sister Mary Jeanne to Robert McCooey, chair of the board of trustees, June 4, 1975, in Parrell, *History of Mercy College*, 28.
123. Parrell, *History of Mercy College*, 20; program for commencement exercises, August 21, 1977, in Parrell, *History of Mercy College*, 37–38.
124. Parrell, *History of Mercy College*, 47, 49.
125. Sister Mary Joannes Christie, "Foreword," in Parrell, *History of Mercy College*, iv; Parrell, *History of Mercy College*, 64.
126. Williams, "Mercy's President"; Progress Report of Mercy College, 1982, 16; *Report to the Commission on Higher Education of the Middle States Association of Colleges and Schools*, April 1994, MCLA, 7; Mercy College Annual Report, 1983–84, MCLA; on Dr. Grunewald's engagement, see *New York Times*, December 14, 1980.
127. Interview with Grunewald, September 24, 2012.
128. *Report to the Commission on Higher Education of the Middle States Association of Colleges and Schools*, April 1994, MCLA, 7; interview with Grunewald, September 24, 2012; Kriss, "Grunewald to Focus on Museum Funds"; Gary

Kriss, "County Budget Cited as Grunewald Quits Museum," *New York Times*, January 19, 1986.

129. Williams, "Mercy's President."

130. Interview with Grunewald, September 24, 2012; Grunewald Linkedin profile; on President Ford's commendation, see *New York Times*, "12 Colleges, 5 in New York Area, Get $10,000 Prizes for Innovation," May 24, 1979.

131. Interview with Grunewald, September 24, 2012.

132. Williams, "Mercy's President"; Mercy College Annual Report, 2008, MCLA, 13.

133. Interview with Grow, October 24, 2012.

134. *Report to the Commission on Higher Education of the Middle States Association of Colleges and Schools*, April 1994, MCLA, 7–8; Justin Hall, "Paving the Way," *Daily Iberian*, September 8, 2010. www.iberianet.com/people/teche_life/paving-the-way/article_7465b4ef-0438-52b8-9aa2-7a03d364e2ca.html.

135. Rhoda Gilinsky, "Ex-Diplomat Outlines Goals for Mercy," *New York Times*, June 30, 1985.

136. Draft Report to the Middle States Commission, 2003, MCLA, 7–8; President's Report, 1987–88, MCLA, 1; *Report to the Commission on Higher Education of the Middle States Association of Colleges and Schools*, April 1994, MCLA, 8.

137. Rhoda Gilinsky, "Remembering Mother," *New York Times*, May 10, 1987.

138. Draft Report to the Middle States Commission, 2003, MCLA, 7–8; *Report to the Commission on Higher Education of the Middle States Association of Colleges and Schools*, April 1994, MCLA; Gilinsky, "Ex-Diplomat Outlines Goals."

139. Bruce Lambert Jr. and Jennifer Preston, "Botnick Admits Lie About Degree," *Newsday*, June 6, 1986.

140. John Fialka, *Sisters, Catholic Nuns and the Making of America* (New York: St. Martin's, 2004); *New York Times*, January 16, 2000; Tara McKelvey, "If You're Thinking of Living in: Dobbs Ferry," *New York Times*, January 24, 1988; *New York Times*, "Town-House Project on Hudson Advances," February 23, 1997.

141. Barbara O'Brien, "Christie Hall Stands as Demolition Plans Stall," *Reporter's Impact*, 1986; Erika Merriam, "Christie Hall Is Falling Down," Mercy College Annual yearbook, 1987, 24–25.

142. President's Report, 1987–88, MCLA, 1–2, 4; Draft Report to the Middle States Commission, 2003, MCLA, 7–8; interview with Grow, October 24, 2012.

143. *Middle States Periodic Review Report*, fall 1983, Sisters of Mercy Archives, 3, in Daigler, *Through the Windows*, 135.

CHAPTER 3

144. Christie, "Foreword," in Parrell, *History of Mercy College*, iv.

145. Elsa Brenner, "Not All Colleges Bemoaning Albany Cuts: Colleges and Less Aid," *New York Times*, March 26, 1995; Mercy College Strategic Plan, 1993, MCLA, 1–2; Draft Report to the Middle States Commission, 2003, MCLA, 8.

146. Interview with Grow, October 24, 2012; Draft Report to the Middle States Commission, 2003, MCLA, 8–9; *Mercy College Periodic Review Report*, June 1999, MCLA, 8–9; Susan Ling, "About Brooklyn: Learning Center as a Melting Pot," *Newsday*, May 7, 1995; Roberta Hershenson, "Helping Bosnian Students Go to School," *New York Times*, August 18, 1996.

147. Dr. Jay Sexter, memorandum to the Mercy College Community, April 26, 1996, MCLA.

148. *New York Times*, "Mercy College Expands to Manhattan," February 14, 1993; interview with Grunewald, September 24, 2012.

149. Penny Singer, "Colleges Aim Courses at Older Students," *New York Times*, September 9, 1991; Joseph Berger, "For Mercy College Teachers: Recruit a Student, Get a Raise," *New York Times*, June 10, 1995; *New York Times*, "For Professors, Phonathon Spells Raise," September 20, 1995.
150. Lynne Ames, "Mercy College Discounts for Jobless," *New York Times*, September 5, 1993; Brenner, "Not All Colleges Bemoaning"; Mercy College Annual Report, 1994–95, MCLA, 3–4; Mercy College Strategic Plan, 1993, MCLA, 12; Draft Report to the Middle States Commission, 2003, MCLA, 10.
151. Brenner, "Not All Colleges Bemoaning."
152. Robert Worth, "Program Spreads to Sing Sing," *New York Times*, June 24, 2001; Abby Ellin, "Cons in Class," *New York Times*, August 3, 2003; Sally Beatty, "Colleges Go Back Behind Bars," *Wall Street Journal*, June 22, 2007.
153. Mercy College Strategic Plan, 1993, MCLA, 8–10, 15; Mercy College Annual Report, 1995–96, MCLA; Draft Report to the Middle States Commission, 2003, MCLA, 9–12.
154. Periodic Review from Mercy College to Middle States, June 2009, MCLA, 8; interview with Grunewald, September 24, 2012; Merri Rosenberg, "LIU Chooses Space at Purchase," *New York Times*, April 2, 2000; Draft Report to the Middle States Commission, 2003, MCLA, 10.
155. Brenner, "Not All Colleges Bemoaning"; Fay Ellis, "Mercy College Offers Acupuncture Training," *New York Times*, October 13, 1996; Donna Greene, "Defining What Makes a Good Teacher," *New York Times*, November 9, 1997; interview with Grunewald, September 24, 2012; Draft Report to the Middle States Commission, 2003, MCLA, 10.
156. Draft Report to the Middle States Commission, 2003, MCLA, 11; Daigler, *Through the Windows*, 136.
157. Draft Report to the Middle States Commission, 2003, MCLA, 12–13.
158. *Journal News*, "Mercy College Names New President," April 24, 1999; Elsa Brenner, "Mercy College Head Extends Her Hand," *New York Times*, September 5, 1999.
159. Draft Report to the Middle States Commission, 2003, MCLA, 13–15; *Journal News*, "Mercy College Aims to Reduce Dropout Rate," June 20, 2000; Elsa Brenner, "Changing of the Guard at Mercy College," *New York Times*, May 23, 2004; Jonathan Lincoln, "Mercy College to Offer Internet-Related Degree," *New York Times*, May 7, 2000.
160. Esther Wermuth and Murray Bromberg, "Mercy's I.C.P. Program Meets the Challenge," *Academic Exchange Quarterly* (Winter 2003): 147–50; Bill Egbert, "College's Teacher Certification Program to Benefit Bronx, NY, Schools," *Daily News*, February 4, 2003.
161. Draft Report to the Middle States Commission, 2003, MCLA, 13–17; Mercy College Annual Report, 2002, MCLA, 11; *Journal News*, "WDFH Gets College Home," June 3, 2001.
162. Elsa Brenner, "New Media Site for Mercy College," *New York Times*, November 11, 2000.
163. *Journal News*, "A Little Disney Magic for Mercy Grads," May 30, 2002; David Herszenhorn, "First Lady Campaigns for Teachers and Trainees," *New York Times*, September 3, 2003; *Newsday*, "Embracing New Teachers: First Lady Lauds Mercy College's National Training Program," September 3, 2003.
164. Edwin McDowell, "Bronx Complex on Site of Former Health Center," *New York Times*, July 2, 2003; C.J. Hughes, "For an Old Hospital, New High-End Uses," *New York Times*, November 24, 2004; Elsa Brenner, "Thriving Corporate Park Spurs Growth in Bronx," *New York Times*, June 15, 2011.

165. *Mercy College Periodic Review Report*, June 1999, MCLA, 14; Donna Greene, "With a Computer, Courses Come to You," *New York Times*, December 26, 1993; Barbara Hines, "Q&A with Mary Lozina," *Education Outlook*, April 10, 2011, 6.
166. Draft Report to the Middle States Commission, 2003, MCLA, 13–17.
167. Interview with Grow, October 24, 2012; Mercy College Annual Report, 2006, MCLA, 17, 18; Draft Report to the Middle States Commission, 2003, MCLA, 17–18.
168. Caitlin Kelly, "Making College a Reality for Hispanic Students," *New York Times*, November 18, 2007; Mercy College Annual Report, 2006, MCLA, 4–5; *Engage: The Magazine from Mercy College* 1, "Mercy College Establishes First Doctoral Program" (Summer/Fall 2007): 5; *Engage: The Magazine from Mercy College* 3 (2008): 7.
169. Mercy College Annual Report, 2006, MCLA, 9; Mercy College Annual Report, 2007, MCLA, 8; *Engage: The Magazine from Mercy College* 1, "A Maverick Move: Mercy Selects New Mascot and Nickname" (Summer/Fall 2007): 3
170. Elsa Brenner, "College's Layoffs: Both Bane and Boon," *New York Times*, June 5, 2005; Mercy College Annual Report, 2007, MCLA, 17.
171. Elzy Kolb, "Madam Presidents," *Westchester Magazine*, March 22, 2011, www.westchestermagazine.com/Westchester-Magazine/April-2011/Madam-Presidents.
172. Mercy College Annual Report, 2008, MCLA, 8; Kolb, "Madam Presidents"; Joan Baum, "College Presidents' Series: President Kimberly Cline, Mercy College," Education Update Online, September/October 2009, www.educationupdate.com/archives/2009/SEP/html/col-preskimb.html.
173. Kolb, "Madam Presidents"; Periodic Review from Mercy College to Middle States, June 2009, 1; Garden City News Online, "College President Appointed to Board of Trustees," July 24, 2009, www.gcnews.com/news/2009-07-24/Community/090.html.
174. Baum, "College Presidents' Series"; *Great Neck Record*, "There's Big News in Higher Education," March 19, 2009; Jennifer Epstein, "Making a Pact," *Inside Higher Ed*, September 4, 2009, www.insidehighered.com/news/2009/09/04/mercy#ixzz1v51MBvnQ; *ADVFN Financial and Company News*, "Mercy College's Pioneering Pact Mentorship Program Shows Gains in Student Retention Rates," November 4, 2010, www.advfn.com/news_Mercy-College-s-Pioneering-Pact-Mentorship-Program-Shows-Gains-in-Student-Rete_45078751.html; Art McFarland, "Mercy Offers One-on-One Mentoring to Freshmen," ABC-7, December 14, 2009, http://abclocal.go.com/wabc/story?section=news/education&id=7157369; Adam Littman, "Mentors Helping Students Find Their Way at College," *New York City Patch*, December 26, 2010, http://newcity.patch.com/articles/mentors-helping-students-find-their-way-at-college; *Garden City Patch*, "Encouraging Educational Advancement through Personalized Mentoring," December 6, 2010, http://gardencity.patch.com/articles/encouraging-educational-advancement-through-personalized-mentoring; AAC&U News, "Advancing Student Success at Mercy College," May 2011, www.aacu.org/aacu_news/aacunews11/may11/feature.cfm; Dr. Kimberly R. Cline, "PACT Mentoring Program Drives Recruitment & Retention," University Business, February 8, 2012, www.universitybusiness.com/news/pact-mentoring-program-drives-recruitment-retention; Periodic Review Mercy Collge to Middle States, June 2009, MCLA, 1.
175. Mercy College Annual Report, 2008, MCLA, 9; Baum, "College Presidents' Series"; *Westchester Herald*, "Mercy College Nursing Program Receives Largest HRSA Grant in Its History," August 3, 2009; *Bronx Times Reporter*, "Mercy College Awarded Grant," August 13, 2009; Mercy College Annual Report, 2009, MCLA, 17.

176. Mercy College press release, "Baroness Pauline Perry Featured Speaker at Gala Opening of Mercy College Center for Global Engagement," November 7, 2011.
177. Mercy College Annual Report, 2010, MCLA, 6; *Wall Street Select*, "Job Growth Surge at Mercy College," November 16, 2010, http://investor.wallstreetselect.com/wss/news/read?GUID=15598457; Jeff Wendt, "Q&A with Deirdre Whitman," Today's Campus Online, April 8, 2010, http://www.todayscampus.com/minute/load.aspx?art=2019&cache=t.
178. Wendt, "Q&A with Deirdre Whitman"; Jeff Wendt, "Q&A with Deirdre Whitman," Today's Campus Online, May 25, 2010, www.todayscampus.com/minute/load.aspx?art=2090&cache=t; Barbara Moroch, "Q&A with Dr. Kimberly R. Cline," *Journal News*, January 13, 2012, available on LoHud, www.lohud.com/apps/pbcs.dll/article?AID=2012120113013&nclick_check=1.
179. *Rivertowns Patch*, "Website Dubs Mercy a 'College of Distinction,'" July 28, 2011, http://rivertowns.patch.com/articles/website-dubs-mercy-a-college-of-distinction; *Hudson Valley Business Journal*, "Mercy College Named 'Military Friendly School' for 2010," August 24, 2009; *Rivertowns Patch*, "From Combat to the Classroom: Mercy College Named Top Military-Friendly School," September 23, 2010, http://rivertowns.patch.com/articles/from-combat-to-the-classroom-mercy-college-named-top-military-friendly-school; *Journal News*, "Mercy College: One to Watch," September 23, 2012; Hines, "Q&A with Mary Lozina," 6.
180. Mercy College Annual Report, 2009, MCLA, 22; Mercy College Annual Report, 2010, MCLA, 22; Mercy College Annual Report, 2011, MCLA, 26; *Evening Times*, "16 Upstate Colleges Set to Receive over $6.7M from Department of Education," May 9, 2012; Patrick Gallagher, "Standard and Poor's Gives Mercy College 'A' Rating," *Westchester County Business Journal*, September 6, 2012.
181. Mercy College Annual Report, 2011, MCLA, 18.
182. *Engage: The Magazine from Mercy College* 6 (Fall 2009), 1; Mercy College Annual Report, 2009, MCLA, 13; *Hudson Valley Business Journal*, "Mercy College Receives $3.5 Million Grant," August 31, 2009; Mercy College Annual Report, 2008, MCLA, 11; *Westchester Herald*, "Mercy College Unveils New Library Learning Commons," October 19, 2009; Lawrence Biemiller, "Campus Architecture Database: Library Learning Commons," *Chronicle of Higher Education*, March 12, 2010.
183. Kristin McGovern, *Impact*, March 2012.
184. *Bronx Times*, November 12, 2009.
185. Mercy College Annual Report, 2008, MCLA, 10.
186. Ibid., 2010, MCLA, 20.
187. Parrell, *History of Mercy College*, 5; Mercy College Annual Report, 2009, MCLA, 9; Patrick Rocchio, "Mercy College Parent Center," *New York Post*, October 7, 2012; Dr. Kimberly Cline, "Mercy College Gives Back Campaign Launch," electronic memorandum to the Mercy College Community, February 22, 2012.
188. Interview with Grunewald, September 24, 2012; Mercy College Annual Report, 2008, MCLA, 13.

CHAPTER 4

189. Mercy College Annual yearbook, 1969, MCLA.
190. Interview with Grow, October 24, 2012.
191. Mercy College Annual yearbooks, 1965–70, MCLA.
192. Ibid.

193. Interview with Grow, October 24, 2012.
194. *Impact*, September 25, 1981, 1.
195. Mercy College Annual yearbook, 1976, MCLA.
196. Ibid., 1965, MCLA.
197. Ibid., 1970, MCLA.
198. Ibid., 1984, MCLA.
199. Interview with Lucretia Mann, October 15, 2012.
200. Interview with Terrance Jackson, October 12, 2012.
201. Interview with Dorothy Balancio, October 14, 2012.
202. Interview with Jose Barzola, October 13, 2012.
203. Interview with Joe Cooke, September 12, 2012.
204. See www.theimpactnews.com.
205. Interview with Doug Otis, December 16, 2012.
206. Ibid.
207. Interview with Michael Perrota, September 15, 2012.
208. Interview with Alan Hartman, October 13, 2012.
209. Interview with Susan Gunser, October 1, 2012.
210. Interview with Adam Parmenter, September 18, 2012.
211. Interview with Rick Sheils, November 28, 2012.
212. Interview with Cooke, September 12, 2012.
213. Interview with Jasmine Dumas, September 12, 2012.
214. Interview with Nicholas Forge, September 12, 2012.
215. Interview with Gloria Schlisselberg, October 11, 2012.
216. Interview with Nick Canzano, October 2012.
217. Interview with Barzola, October 13, 2012.
218. Ibid.
219. Interview with Cooke, September 12, 2012.
220. Parrell, *History of Mercy College*, 37, 57–58.
221. Mercy College Annual yearbooks, 1984 and 1988, MCLA; *Impact*, October 17, 1990, 1.
222. *Impact*, October 2005, 1.
223. Ibid., April 2006, 1, 7.
224. Interview with Louis Grasso, November 15, 2012.

CHAPTER 5

225. Interview with Neil Judge, October 20, 2012.
226. Mercy College Department of Athletics.
227. See www.eccsports.org.
228. Interview with Neil Judge, October 25, 2012.
229. *Impact*, November 2012, 1.
230. Parrell, *History of Mercy College*, 39.
231. Interview with Judge, October 20, 2012.
232. Mercy College Department of Athletics.
233. Ibid.
234. Interview with Judge, October 20, 2012.
235. Ibid.
236. Mercy College Annual yearbook, 1984, MCLA.
237. *Impact*, March 14, 1983, 8.
238. Mercy College Department of Athletics.
239. *Impact*, March 18, 1996, 8.

240. Mercy College Department of Athletics.
241. Interview with Neil Judge, November 8, 2012.
242. *Impact*, April 26, 1989, 8.
243. Mercy College Department of Athletics.
244. Interview with Darryl Bullock, December 19, 2012.
245. Ibid.
246. *New York Times*, December 26, 2004.
247. Interview with Bullock, December 19, 2012.
248. Mercy College Department of Athletics.
249. *Impact*, November 21, 1989, 8.
250. Ibid., November 24, 1993, 8.
251. Mercy College Department of Athletics.
252. See NCAA Volleyball at http://fs.ncaa.org/Docs/stats/fall_champs_records/2001/volleyball_w.pdf.
253. Mercy College Department of Athletics.
254. Ibid.
255. *Impact*, April 18, 1983, 8.
256. Ibid., May 9, 1990, 16.
257. Interview with Jim Thompson, November 25, 2012.
258. Mercy College Department of Athletics.
259. *Impact*, May 1, 1990, 12.
260. Mercy College Department of Athletics.
261. Ibid.
262. Ibid.
263. Ibid.
264. Ibid.
265. See www.mercyathletics.com.

Index

J

K

L

M

N

Y

Z

About the Authors

Eric Martone is assistant professor of social studies education at Mercy College. He has a PhD in global history from Stony Brook University, an MA in European history from Western Connecticut State University, an MA in global history from Iona College and a BA in history from Pace University. Before beginning his career in higher education, he was a secondary social studies teacher in Connecticut. In 2011, he received the John Rogers Memorial Award from the Connecticut Education Association in recognition of his leading contributions in the areas of education and scholarship. He has published dozens of articles, many of which have appeared in such journals as the *Journal of Global History* and the *International Social Science Review*, and his research has received financial support from such organization as the National Endowment for the Humanities and the American Historical Association. His most recent books include *The Black Musketeer: Reevaluating Alexandre Dumas within the Francophone World* (2011) and the *Encyclopedia of Blacks in European History and Culture* (2009).

Michael Perrota is assistant professor of media studies at Mercy College. He has an MFA in professional writing from Western Connecticut State University, an MS in journalism from Iona College and a BS in marketing from Pace University. He has been a news reporter, a sports editor and a feature writer for various weekly and daily newspapers in New Jersey for the past decade. For six years, he worked in the sports department at the *Newark Star-Ledger*. He has won four New Jersey Press

Association Awards, including the Lloyd P. Burns Award for Responsible Journalism. He is also the advisor to the Mercy College newspaper, the *Impact*. Since he has become its advisor, the paper has won various awards, including first-place awards in news reporting from the New York Press Association and Scholastic Press Association.

www.ingramcontent.com/pod-product-compliance
Lightning Source LLC
Chambersburg PA
CBHW070356100426
42812CB00005B/1527

* 9 7 8 1 5 4 0 2 3 2 1 6 8 *